JAILHOUSE INFORMANTS

PSYCHOLOGY AND CRIME
General Editors: Brian Bornstein, University of Nebraska, and Monica Miller, University of Nevada, Reno

The Perversion of Youth: Controversies in the Assessment and Treatment of Juvenile Sex Offenders
Frank C. DiCataldo

Jury Decision Making: The State of the Science
Dennis J. Devine

Deviant and Criminal Behavior in the Workplace
Edited by Steven M. Elias

Psychopathy: An Introduction to Biological Findings and Their Implications
Andrea L. Glenn and Adrian Raine

Gender, Psychology, and Justice: The Mental Health of Women and Girls in the Legal System
Edited by Corinne C. Datchi and Julie R. Ancis

Criminal Trials and Mental Disorders
Thomas L. Hafemeister

Criminal Trajectories: A Developmental Perspective
David M. Day and Margit Wiesner

Understanding Police Interrogation: Confessions and Consequences
William Douglas Woody and Krista D. Forrest

Understanding Eyewitness Memory: Theory and Applications
Sean M. Lane and Kate A. Houston

Jailhouse Informants: Psychological and Legal Perspectives
Jeffrey S. Neuschatz and Jonathan M. Golding

Jailhouse Informants

Psychological and Legal Perspectives

Jeffrey S. Neuschatz *and* Jonathan M. Golding

NEW YORK UNIVERSITY PRESS
New York

NEW YORK UNIVERSITY PRESS
New York
www.nyupress.org

© 2022 by New York University
All rights reserved

References to Internet websites (URLs) were accurate at the time of writing. Neither the author nor New York University Press is responsible for URLs that may have expired or changed since the manuscript was prepared.

Library of Congress Cataloging-in-Publication Data
Names: Neuschatz, Jeffrey S., author. | Golding, Jonathan M., author.
Title: Jailhouse informants : psychological and legal perspectives / Jeffrey S. Neuschatz and Jonathan M. Golding.
Description: New York : New York University Press, [2022] | Series: Psychology and crime | Includes bibliographical references and index.
Identifiers: LCCN 2021025528 | ISBN 9781479803309 (hardback) | ISBN 9781479803316 (paperback) | ISBN 9781479803354 (ebook) | ISBN 9781479803330 (ebook other)
Subjects: LCSH: Evidence, Criminal—United States—Psychological aspects. | Informers—Legal status, laws, etc.—United States. | Prisoners—Legal status, laws, etc.—United States.
Classification: LCC KF9665 .N48 2022 | DDC 345.73/06—dc23
LC record available at https://lccn.loc.gov/2021025528

New York University Press books are printed on acid-free paper, and their binding materials are chosen for strength and durability. We strive to use environmentally responsible suppliers and materials to the greatest extent possible in publishing our books.

Manufactured in the United States of America

10 9 8 7 6 5 4 3 2 1

Also available as an ebook

We dedicate the book to some very important people in our lives. I (Jeff) dedicate this book to my brother, Kevin, who has always had more confidence and ambition for me than I have had in myself. He has always pushed me to achieve more than I thought I could. I owe much of my success to his confidence in me. Kevin, I am grateful to have you as a brother and advocate.

For me (Jonathan), I dedicate this book to my wife Roni for her unconditional support.

CONTENTS

Introduction: Psychological Perspectives on Jailhouse Informants — 1

1. Jailhouse Informants throughout History — 17
2. Legal Perspectives on Admitting Jailhouse Informant Testimony — 37
3. Confession Evidence: Is It Valid? — 56
4. Detecting Deception — 76
5. Perceptions of Jailhouse Informants in the Courtroom — 98
6. Expert Testimony, Cross-Examination, and Judicial Instructions — 123

Conclusion: Recommendations Concerning Jailhouse Informant Testimony — 149

Acknowledgments — 165

Notes — 167

Bibliography — 169

Index — 185

About the Authors — 195

Introduction

Psychological Perspectives on Jailhouse Informants

Between ten and eleven o'clock the night of November 3, 1979, John McGinest (aged twenty-five) was shot and killed in Long Beach, California. A police investigation led to several eyewitnesses who stated that the shooter was a Black or Hispanic man. A subsequent photo lineup shown to six eyewitnesses did not lead to the identification of the shooter. The police, however, showed one eyewitness a photo of a white man, Thomas Goldstein, for a second time. This eyewitness stated that it was possible that Goldstein had committed the murder. Based on this "identification" Goldstein, an ex-Marine, Vietnam vet, and engineering student who lived near the murder scene, was arrested. In jail, Goldstein was housed in a cell with Edward (Eddie) Fink, a police informant for many years who had received incentives for informing on his cellmates in the past. The day after being put in the cell together, Fink informed police that Goldstein had confessed to him about murdering McGinest (Possley, 2012).

Despite the lack of physical or forensic evidence (e.g., the murder weapon was never found) linking Goldstein to McGinest's murder, Goldstein was brought to trial in 1980 in Los Angeles County Superior Court. The prosecution based their case on the testimony of the eyewitness mentioned above and the jailhouse informant Fink. On the stand Fink testified that Goldstein confessed to the murder. In addition, Fink lied, stating that he had received no incentives for testifying, although he had charges dropped in exchange. Besides this testimony, the prosecution's theory (although unsupported by any evidence) was that Goldstein murdered McGinest because McGinest owed him money. Goldstein was convicted by the jury and sentenced to twenty-five years to life in prison (Possley, 2012).

Following his conviction Goldstein filed numerous appeals—none was successful. However, in 1990 a grand jury report revealed that between 1979 and 1990 prosecutors in Los Angeles County often presented false testimony by jailhouse informants. This report led Goldstein to track down a lawyer who had information showing that Fink had presented such false testimony and was compensated for it. In 2000 the eyewitness in the trial recanted their testimony about Goldstein, and in November 2002 Goldstein's conviction was overturned in district court. The court ruled that Goldstein had been deprived of a fair trial because the prosecution failed to reveal that Fink's testimony led to him receiving benefits, thereby depriving Goldstein of a chance to impeach Fink's testimony. An appeal by the prosecution heard by the US Court of Appeals for the Ninth Circuit in December 2003 upheld the district court's decision, overturning Goldstein's conviction and granting him a new trial. Although the court ordered Goldstein's immediate release, prosecutors did not comply. They turned Goldstein over to county jailers, who technically were not covered by the court order. It took until April 2004 for a judge to rule that the eyewitness's testimony from 1980 could not be used in a retrial. The prosecution finally dismissed the case and Goldstein was released (Possley, 2012).

Fink was also used by the prosecution in the case of *People v. Thompson* (1988), one of the most egregious cases of prosecutorial misconduct. Thomas Thompson and his roommate, David Leitch, were both arrested and tried separately for the rape and murder of Ginger Fleischli. At the preliminary hearing for Thompson's trial, the prosecution produced several jailhouse informants who testified that Thompson had confessed that Leitch hired him to murder Fleischli. The prosecution believed that Leitch wanted Fleischli dead because she was interfering with Leitch reconciling with a former lover. Yet by the time of the trial, the prosecution had disregarded this theory and the jailhouse informants in favor of a new theory in which Thompson acted alone in killing Fleischli. The prosecution then found two different jailhouse informants to confirm this new story. One of these new jailhouse informants was Fink.

At Thompson's trial Fink adhered to the prosecution's theory and testified that Thompson admitted to him that he had murdered Fleischli and that he had acted alone; Leitch was not there when the crime occurred. Based primarily on Fink's and another jailhouse informant's testimony, Thompson was convicted of murder and sentenced to death. For his efforts, Fink was released from jail shortly after testifying (Minsker, 2009). During Leitch's trial (he was sentenced to fifteen years in prison for his role in the murder), the prosecutor returned to his original theory that Leitch and Fleischli had been dating and Leitch decided to murder her due to her interference with a past relationship of his. Leitch testified at a hearing that he told police in 1981 that he witnessed Thompson and Fleischli have consensual sex on the night in question. This was of course incompatible with the rape-murder theory the prosecution put forward during Thompson's initial trial. Despite this inconsistency, Thompson was executed in 1998 after spending seventeen years in prison.

As will become clear throughout this book, there was nothing exceptional about Fink or the dubious outcomes of cases in which he offered testimony—he is a prototypical jailhouse informant (Moxley, 2015). Moreover, these cases illustrate the influence that the testimony of jailhouse informants (also referred to as "snitches," "rats," "finks," "rat finks," "stool pigeons," "pigeons," and "in-custody informants") can have in the courtroom. A jailhouse informant is an inmate (typically male) who (a) claims that he has learned information from a defendant (who was unknown to him prior to incarceration) during a conversation or through overhearing the defendant speak with someone else, (b) informs or is asked by a prosecutor (in most cases) about his apparent knowledge, and (c) testifies about this evidence in court. Given that the context of receiving information (i.e., jail) does not typically involve a crime itself, the relationship between a jailhouse informant and a criminal (i.e., strangers), and the fact that jailhouse informants testify in court, they are unique compared to other types of informants in how they benefit the legal system. The latter includes accomplices (coconspirators who typically know one another) and confidential informants typically working with the police (see Natapoff, 2009) who receive inside information, often at the time a crime occurred. The purpose of this book is to offer a greater understanding of jailhouse informants, how often they are used in the criminal court system, the influence of their testimony, and their relation to false convictions. We cover historical and legal issues surrounding jailhouse informants, but at its core this book examines the psychology of jailhouse informants, including (a) why an individual would become a jailhouse informant, (b) why jailhouse informants are sometimes willing to deceive the court, (c) the impact of jailhouse informants (sometimes quite harmful) in court, and (d) attempts to attenuate the impact of false jailhouse informant testimony.

Jailhouse informants are particularly persuasive to jurors. Research has shown that when such a "snitch" testifies on behalf of the prosecution, there is more likely to be a guilty verdict than when such testimony is not presented (Neuschatz et al., 2008). When informant testimony is included in a trial, there are even as many guilty verdicts returned as when defendants themselves offered an incriminating confession to the police (Wetmore et al., 2014). Not only is the testimony of jailhouse informants particularly influential, but it is also a leading contributor to wrongful convictions. Informants, after all, are generally criminals offering testimony in return for a reduced sentence or another benefit. As convicts who see testimony as a means to gain something they want, they may be unreliable purveyors of the truth.

As one might imagine, the fact that jailhouse informants may reveal critical information does not mean that they are acting out of altruism, compassion for the victims and their family, or a sense of justice. Instead, jailhouse informants understand that the information they hold can make or break a case. Therefore, they typically testify only if there is an incentive or reward from the prosecution on offer (see Los Angeles County Grand Jury, 1990). The incentive or reward can vary, but jailhouse informants can be granted reduced jail time, receive money, have their legal immigration status changed favorably (see Natapoff, 2009), receive more privileges in jail, or even have payments made to a third party (Los Angeles County Grand Jury, 1990). Moreover, jurors may not even be aware that the jailhouse informant is testifying in exchange for a reward. For example, the prosecution in a case is typically under no obligation to "seal the deal" with jailhouse informants before they testify (Covey, 2014; Natapoff, 2018). In fact, jailhouse informants may receive a reward *after* their courtroom testimony, which means that they can truthfully declare on the stand that they have not received anything in exchange for testifying.

Do prosecutors care that jailhouse informants are inmates? It seems not, given that prosecutors have appeared more than willing to offer incentives to jailhouse informants and that their number does not appear to be decreasing, even though research has shown that overturned convictions are sometimes based on false testimony from jailhouse informants (Covey, 2014). Thus, it appears that the status of a jailhouse informant as a convicted or accused criminal who might reasonably be assumed to be less than credible is less important to a prosecutor than the fact that they might help the state win a case.

Testimony offered by a jailhouse informant is viewed as a *secondary confession* (Neuschatz et al., 2008). A jailhouse informant is not the primary source of a confession but offers the confession secondhand. For example, take the case of Alfred Swinton, convicted of murder in Connecticut and sentenced to sixty years partly because of the testimony of a jailhouse informant who claimed Swinton confessed to him. Swinton served nineteen years but was released after exculpatory DNA and other forensic evidence was uncovered. In jailhouse informant cases, the defendant (serving as a "declarant") is said to have directly confessed to the jailhouse informant or the informant overhears the defendant confess to someone else and testifies about the declarant's confession.

The admissibility of such testimony is bolstered by the courts (*Hoffa v. US*, 1966; see also Fessinger et al., 2020), which assume that the legal system has safeguards that will prevent unreliable jailhouse informant testimony from leading to a false conviction. These safeguards include cross-examination, instructions to juries (Wetmore, Neuschatz, Fessinger, et al., 2020), the requirement that prosecutors disclose any incentives offered to jailhouse informants in exchange for testimony (e.g., *Giglio v. US*, 1972), and defense attorneys' power to request expert testimony to counter jailhouse informant testimony (*Daubert v. Merrell Dow Pharmaceuticals*, 1993). In addition, it can be argued that the safeguards against the wholesale use of jailhouse informant testimony are protected by several US Supreme Court rulings that specify the situations in which informant testimony is allowed. For example, jailhouse informants can testify only if they did not deliberately elicit the information from another prisoner (*Massiah v. US*, 1964) and are not allowed to testify about information they gained from their cellmates as the result of a threat (*Arizona v. Fulminante*, 1991).

Despite the above safeguards, allowing jailhouse informants to testify has become controversial (see Joy, 2007). On the one hand, Natapoff (2009) has argued that informants "are a potent and sometimes necessary crime-fighting tool" (p. 2), and the judicial system can benefit enormously from jailhouse informant testimony. For example, jailhouse informants can expose prosecutors to crimes and can provide information about known crimes to prosecutors that they would not normally have access to. Yet on the other hand, jailhouse informants are not always reliable or accurate—there is evidence showing that they are more than willing to provide false information to juries (Garrett, 2011). This has predictably led to a relatively high percentage of false convictions of innocent individuals, allowing the true perpetrator to remain free and potentially commit other crimes. The inclusion of false evidence during cases also undermines the adversarial system of the courtroom, which requires reliable evidence (Joy, 2007).

Examples of jailhouse informants providing false testimony continue to accumulate. According to the Innocence Project (2019), the leading contributing factors in wrongful convictions are (in descending order) eyewitness misidentification, faulty forensic evidence, false confessions, and the use of informants. In an examination of 250 DNA exoneration cases, Garrett (2011) found that in 28 of them a jailhouse informant had provided testimony at trial. Moreover, the Center for Wrongful Convictions discovered that informants were involved in 45.9 percent of 111 capital cases, making false informant testimony the leading known cause of wrongful conviction in US capital cases since the reinstatement of the death penalty (Warden, 2004). Also, the National Registry of Exonerations found that jailhouse informants have contributed to over 119 known wrongful convictions, which included 102 murder cases (Gross & Jackson, 2015). It is important to note that not only the sheer number of cases involving jailhouse informants and false convictions but also that jurors are so willing to be persuaded by jailhouse informant testimony are alarming. Yet their testimony continues to be widely utilized. The most extensive report to date concerning the use of jailhouse informant testimony, conducted by the Los Angeles County Grand Jury (1990), found that prosecutors used informants in 233 murder and felony cases in the Los Angeles area over a ten-year period (1979–1989).

The prosecutorial use of jailhouse informants raises two critical issues. First, jailhouse informants are generally employed in the most serious cases—rape and murder—when there is very little evidence other than their testimony (see Neuschatz et al., 2020). Second, there is no accounting of the number of jailhouse informants. In fact, one could argue that the number of potential jailhouse informants is equal to the number of inmates since any inmate could potentially "snitch" on another inmate. As Natapoff (2009) notes, inmates are surrounded by a steady stream of vulnerable targets whom they can take advantage of. The incentives are always available, and being in jail educates inmates about informing—that is, learning how to obtain information about crimes from various sources.

Characteristics of Jailhouse Informants

The most thorough investigation of jailhouse informants to date, the Los Angeles County Grand Jury (1990), offers some help in understanding the dynamics surrounding the continued use of jailhouse informant testimony. The report found that jailhouse informants were most often incarcerated men facing a lengthy prison sentence who tended to reoffend, were highly motivated to curry favor with the authorities, were not committed to the truth, were motivated to serve their own interests, and had previously testified for the prosecution as jailhouse informants in trials involving other defendants. One conclusion was very clear from the report: "Jailhouse informants want some benefit in return for testimony" (Los Angeles County Grand Jury, 1990, p. 11). The jailhouse informants were clearly not testifying because of some moral imperative to protect society from crime; they conspired with law enforcement to testify only because it served their own self-interest. In this context, one must remember that jailhouse informants are generally under enormous pressure to cooperate with authorities. As suspects in criminal cases or convicted criminals, they are threatened with long sentences. One of their only options to avoid jail time or gain privileges is to work with prosecutors and gain some type of incentive.

The conclusions of the Los Angeles County Grand Jury (1990) have been largely supported by recent content analyses of DNA exoneration cases involving jailhouse informants (Garrett, 2011; Neuschatz et al., 2020). In one of these analyses, Neuschatz et al. examined the first twenty-two trials recorded by the Innocence Project that contained at least one jailhouse informant or cooperating witness and led to a DNA exoneration. The authors defined an informant as someone who claimed to have obtained evidence about the defendant's case while incarcerated (i.e., a jailhouse informant) or someone (not incarcerated) who learned about the case through some connection with the defendant or through his own experiences but who required an incentive to testify (i.e., cooperating witness). In total, the sample consisted of fifty-three informants (forty-three jailhouse informants and ten cooperating witnesses). It is important to note that the authors focused exclusively on wrongful conviction cases overturned by incontrovertible DNA evidence, which means that these cases provided known examples of informants providing demonstrably false incriminating testimony in court (excluding informants who testified for the defense). Because only cases in which DNA evidence was preserved were reviewed, they may not encompass all those in which jailhouse informants testified.

Of the fifty-three, thirty-four jailhouse informants testified for the prosecution against twenty-eight defendants. These jailhouse informants were like those described in the Los Angeles County Grand Jury (1990). As would be expected, nearly all prosecution witnesses had previous run-ins with the law and extensive criminal histories. Only nine were asked during trial if they had ever previously testified for the prosecution. Most of the jailhouse informants were incarcerated for nonviolent crimes (68.75 percent); these included crimes that did not involve a weapon during the commission of the crime (e.g., burglary, theft; 50.00 percent), crimes that involve deceit (e.g., perjury, fraud; 12.50 percent), or both (6.25 percent).

Relatively few jailhouse informants (21 percent) were in jail for violent crimes (e.g., murder, sexual assault). All the defendants, on the other hand, were convicted of violent crimes in the case in which the jailhouse informant testified, including four for murder, six for rape, and eighteen for both murder and rape. While jailhouse informants are often used in prosecuting major crimes such as murder and rape, and despite the sample examined in the Neuschatz et al. study, it would be misleading to suggest that these are the only cases that they testify in.

Jailhouse Informants' Motivations to Testify

As far as why the jailhouse informants in the Neuschatz et al. (2020) study testified, it must be recalled that one of the conclusions of the Los Angeles County Grand Jury (1990) was that jailhouse informants testify only to serve their own interests. Thus, it is not surprising that a content analysis of the trials by Neuschatz et al. (2020) revealed that almost every jailhouse informant was questioned about their motivation for testifying (such as any deal they may be receiving). In fact, twenty-eight of thirty-two prosecution jailhouse informants were questioned by either the prosecution (71.43 percent) or the defense (75 percent) about whether they were provided any incentive. Most prosecution jailhouse informants (75 percent) explicitly denied receiving anything, and only 12.50 percent admitted that they were receiving an incentive in exchange for their testimony. As an example of the latter, one jailhouse informant indicated that the prosecutor promised he would serve only one year in prison for his conviction of unarmed robbery as opposed to five years, the standard sentence for this class of felony in the state in which the crime occurred (*People v. Wyniemko*, 1994, p. WYN-000333).

The promise of getting out of prison early was not the only motive the informants claimed to have. There were eighteen informants who were asked directly why they had decided to come forward to testify, 80 percent of whom claimed that they came forward for some greater good such as wanting to do the right thing, feeling bad for the family, or believing that the defendant was a threat to society (Neuschatz et al., 2020). For example, one prosecution jailhouse informant stated, "It's something I'm doing as a man. I feel it's the right thing to do" (*People v. Restivo*, 1986, p. RHK-014802). In the psychology literature, this type of altruistic motive for testifying has been referred to as a dispositional motive (DeLoach et al., 2020).

When jailhouse informants provide dispositional reasons for testifying, it may lead jurors to commit fundamental attribution error (FAE). FAE refers to the tendency to overestimate dispositional factors and underestimate situational factors when explaining another person's behavior (Ross, 1977). Therefore, when evaluating a jailhouse informant's motives for testifying, jurors will typically identify dispositional reasons (e.g., trying to do the right thing) rather than relying on situational factors (e.g., incentives). As we will see, the more that a jury attributes a jailhouse informant's motives to dispositional reasons, the greater the likelihood the jury will have more positive feelings toward the informant, trust their testimony, and vote guilty (see DeLoach et al., 2020; Wetmore, Neuschatz, Fessinger, et al., 2020).

Jailhouse Informant Testimony

Neuschatz et al.'s (2020) content analysis of informants also revealed a number of trends in jailhouse informant testimony that were not addressed in the Los Angeles County Grand Jury. Specifically, the analysis of cases exonerated by DNA revealed that while informant testimony contained important true details of the crime, the informants' testimony was often inconsistent and prosecutors made attempts to bolster the reliability of the informants to alleviate jurors' concerns regarding the informants' criminal histories. On average, 66.95 percent of the details disclosed by the prosecution informants were verifiably accurate. For instance, four prosecution jailhouse informants (14.29 percent of twenty-eight available) testified to one or more specific details that were confidential and not released to the public. It is important to remember that these were all DNA exoneration cases—the innocent defendants in these cases could not have known any of these privileged details.

How could the informants have known the details of specific cases? The answer is that it is not as difficult as one might assume to obtain crime-related facts to fabricate a confession with accurate details. As we will see, a resourceful inmate may use friends, family, the TV or Internet, corrupt police officers, or corrupt prison guards to gather such information. There are also networks of jailhouse informants, through which inmates buy and sell information that is then used to fabricate a detailed and factually accurate testimony (Covey, 2014; Natapoff, 2009). In addition, the police or prosecutor, during an interview, may intentionally or unintentionally leak confidential information to the jailhouse informants through the questions they ask (Garrett, 2011; Roberts, 2005; Roth, 2016). Thus, there are a variety of ways in which jailhouse informants can obtain information not released to the public.

The fact that jailhouse informants have undisclosed information about a crime, regardless of how it was obtained, is problematic in the courtroom for at least two important reasons. First, privileged information presented by a jailhouse informant bolsters the informant's credibility as jurors are left to search for alternative sources of the information (i.e., not from the defendant himself). Prior research has shown that people are not particularly skilled at looking for alternative explanations and are likely to fall prey to prosecutorial bias (Wetmore, Neuschatz, Fessinger, et al., 2020). In other words, jurors may assume that the prosecutor has properly vetted the witness before trial and would not allow dishonest testimony. Accordingly, jurors may uncritically accept that jailhouse informant testimony was truly obtained from a defendant and that this information must be accurate. Second, a jailhouse informant will typically weave accurate details into a false story. We should note that it is very difficult for most jurors to detect fabricated testimony. As pointed out by Vrij et al. (2010; noted in chapter 4), successfully detecting lies is an inherently difficult task that becomes more challenging when the lies are embedded in an otherwise truthful account. Therefore, if a jailhouse informant's testimony generally fits a fact pattern, then detecting false information will be immensely difficult for jurors. The result of this interweaving of true and false information is that a jailhouse informant's testimony is likely to be extremely persuasive to jurors (Garrett, 2011; Neuschatz et al., 2020).

In addition to testifying about nonpublic details, the content analysis in Neuschatz et al. (2020) revealed that jailhouse informants' statements often contained inconsistencies. For example, 55.6 percent of informants would incorrectly state a particular murder weapon was used. Additionally, discrepancies were found between their testimony and what they had previously reported to the police or prosecutor (50 percent) as well as between their current testimony and testimony they had given in the past (e.g., at pretrial hearings; 50 percent). These findings may not be viewed as surprising when one considers that the jailhouse informants' testimony was from cases that eventually resulted in DNA exonerations.

An additional way to gauge the importance of jailhouse informant testimony in court was examined by Neuschatz et al. (2020). It was determined how often jailhouse informant testimony was mentioned by the prosecution in closing arguments. Not surprisingly, the prosecution referred to the statements made by jailhouse informants in 94.74 percent (based on the nineteen trials available) of the trials during closing statements. Not only did the prosecution mention the testimony of the jailhouse informant, but statements by the prosecution also bolstered the informant's credibility and promoted trust in the informant. For example, in one case the prosecution argued that the fact that the informant had previously testified several times in other cases against defendants was an indication of his honesty (*People v. Gray*, 1978, p. GRAD-000305). Not only did the prosecution bolster the credibility of the jailhouse informant's testimony, but in 78.95 percent of the cases (based on nineteen available), the prosecution presented reasons unrelated to the facts of the case that promoted the truthfulness of the jailhouse informant's testimony. For instance, the prosecution frequently used the jailhouse informant's criminal past as another indication that the informant was being truthful on the witness stand. In *State v. Hernandez* (1985, p. HERN-008418–HERN-008419), the prosecution argued that the fact that the jailhouse informant was truthful about his past criminal record was evidence that his testimony against the defendant was also truthful.

A final point should be noted about the Innocence Project's DNA exoneration cases. Kassin et al. (2012) found that most false confessions in these cases also contained multiple trial errors such as false identification, faulty forensic science, and prosecutorial misconduct. Similarly, cases containing jailhouse informants were also riddled with trial errors (Neuschatz et al., 2020). Neuschatz et al. found that the average number of contributing causes to the wrongful convictions in these exoneration cases was 2.68 (1.68 when excluding the jailhouse informant as a factor). After the use of jailhouse informants, which necessarily occurred in every case due to the focus of Neuschatz et al., the second leading contributor was unvalidated testimony involving improper forensic evidence (in twelve cases) and eyewitness misidentification (in eight cases). It is worth noting that every case had more than one contributing factor leading to a conviction.

Given the danger of a jailhouse informant providing false testimony in court, the criminal justice system faces the daunting task of determining when jailhouse informant testimony is true versus false. One could argue that the justice system faces this problem with all witnesses and that determining whether any witness is being truthful is particularly difficult, especially since individuals are often convinced by factors that do not indicate the truth (see Vrij, 2008). However, jailhouse informants add to this problem because they are, for the most part, practiced liars who have used their skills at deception to successfully obtain incentives in the past. For example, as noted, jailhouse informants are adept at testifying about events that match factual patterns. The information they may present is accurate, but it was obtained not from a fellow inmate but from publicly available sources. In fact, jailhouse informants may testify about true events with the only potential lie being the source of their information. Besides the difficulty in detecting deception, jailhouse informants have the upper hand in a courtroom because jurors typically believe that prosecutors have already vetted the witness and determined that their testimony is truthful (see Wetmore, Neuschatz, Roth, et al., 2020). To summarize, a jailhouse informant in the courtroom presents a real challenge to the fairness of a case because these witnesses often unreasonably tip the balance toward the prosecution, leaving defense attorneys powerless against their testimony (see Joy, 2007).

The Present Book

This book offers a broad understanding of jailhouse informant testimony, historically, legally, and psychologically. It draws on both psychological research and the legal literature to address how jailhouse informants are used, the percentage of cases that have ultimately been overturned on other evidence, how such informants are perceived in the courtroom, and means by which jurors might be informed about the risks of their testimony, ideally leading to fewer false convictions. This is a topic that has significant real-world effects on justice, though relatively little has been published on it. No other book has specifically examined the issue of jailhouse informants, although Alexandra Natapoff's (2009) volume, *Snitching: Criminal Informants and the Erosion of American Justice*, does broach the issue. However, the Natapoff book focuses on "street" (confidential) informants, is primarily a legal resource, offers almost no coverage of the psychological components of jailhouse informant testimony, and includes no presentation of jailhouse informant research. There are a wide variety of other types of publications about jailhouse informants (e.g., Covey, 2014; Goforth, 2019; Natapoff, 2018), but none of these has the length or depth of treatment as this book.

Regarding the psychological influence of jailhouse informant testimony in the courtroom, recent psychology and law research shows that jailhouse informant testimony leads to more guilty verdicts than when such testimony is not presented (Maeder & Pica, 2014; Maeder & Yamamoto, 2017; Neuschatz et al., 2008; Neuschatz et al., 2012; Wetmore et al., 2014). In addition, Wetmore et al. (2014) found that jailhouse informant testimony led to as many guilty verdicts as an incriminating confession made by a defendant to the police. Moreover, mock jurors are swayed by jailhouse informant testimony even when they are aware of the incentive the jailhouse informant received for testifying (Neuschatz et al., 2008) and even when they are given explicit cautionary instructions to discount the testimony (Wetmore, Neuschatz, Fessinger, et al., 2020). Thus, not only is jailhouse informant testimony influential, but, as we have discussed, it may lead to false convictions.

This book provides an overview of jailhouse informant research from the fields of psychology and law as well as related research (e.g., confessions, lying). Chapter 1 discusses the use of jailhouse informant testimony in historical perspective. This chapter includes data on how often and in what cases jailhouse informant testimony is used, demographics of jailhouse informants, outcomes, and overturned verdicts. Chapter 2 reviews the legal status of jailhouse informant testimony and summarizes various legal opinions and court decisions about jailhouse informants in the United States.

The next four chapters explore the vast amount of psychological research pertinent to jailhouse informant testimony. Chapter 3 covers confessions. It is critical to discuss the psychology of confessions since, as noted above, by definition a jailhouse informant testifies about information allegedly confessed to him by a defendant. This chapter leads directly to a discussion of lying, the focus of chapter 4. We discuss theories and research on how individuals lie and reasons for lying, and we examine how both laypeople and police officers are poor at detecting deception because they tend to rely on cues that are not indicative of lying. Chapter 5 covers psychology and law research investigating the perception of jailhouse informants in court (i.e., legal decision making), making clear the influence that jailhouse informant testimony can have on jurors in a courtroom (Neuschatz et al., 2008). Our coverage of psychological research ends with chapter 6. In this chapter we present research that has investigated potential safeguards (expert testimony, cross-examination, and judicial instructions) against false testimony in the courtroom, including jailhouse informant testimony. In addition to presenting this research, we evaluate whether the limited psychological research suggests that such remedies will prove successful.

The book concludes with an examination of legal remedies to the impact of jailhouse informants; for example, some states have amended their laws to allow for specific jailhouse informant instructions, and several legal commentators have suggested reforms such as pretrial credibility hearings. There is an urgent need to understand the influence of jailhouse informants and how their testimony can best be handled in court in the interests of justice. We offer recommendations for best practices in dealing with jailhouse informant testimony in court.

1

Jailhouse Informants throughout History

The history of jailhouse informants is long, inglorious, and filled with colorful and disreputable characters (Bloom, 2002; Marr, 1971; Zimmerman, 1994). Both ancient and modern jailhouse informants were largely interested in benefiting themselves. Even though they might have offered true information, almost all jailhouse informants had been caught breaking the law and informed on their friends and colleagues to avoid punishment. As will become clear, this issue was problematic for courts and is likely why English courts adopted a corroboration rule, in which jury members were cautioned about convicting on the sole basis of the testimony of a cooperating witness. Throughout this historical overview it is necessary to discuss cooperating witnesses—that is, anyone working with the authorities—and to not set apart those who work with law officers after learning about information in jail (i.e., jailhouse informants). It is not clear that there was a sharp distinction between different types of informants (i.e., accomplices, cooperating informants, and jailhouse informants) for the court system in the ancient or medieval world—an informant was an informant regardless of where or how the information was obtained. Later in the chapter we will discuss that distinguishing jailhouse informants from other informants occurred much later historically, one reason being that jails have most often been used to detain individuals in the modern era (US Bureau of Justice Statistics, 1984, 2020). In our historical review we will examine the histories of many different types of cooperating witnesses but mostly focus on accomplice witnesses. We do so because we believe they set the stage for the modern category of jailhouse informants.

In this chapter, we review the first known informers, who hailed from ancient Greece (for historical reviews, see Bloom, 2002; Marr, 1971; Zimmerman, 1994). Next, we will examine the Middle Ages and how the informer system grew into two distinct subsystems: approver and common informer. Approvers were convicted of felonies and were expected to inform on their accomplices, whereas a common informer was someone who reported only minor infractions. This system was adopted by the English court. We will then move to a description of the colorful French detective Eugène-François Vidocq, who was a former deserter, a criminal, a womanizer, and later a detective (sometimes referred to as the first detective). Vidocq was an important figure known not only for his colorful personality but also because he was the first police officer to use a network of informants to solve crimes—a practice that was quickly adopted by the United Kingdom's Scotland Yard. This was the beginning of what we now see as the modern-day informant system. Finally, we review some of the landmark cases and scandals involving informants in recent times.

The Ancient Informer

The history of informers most likely dates to the beginning of organized government. Bloom (2002) argued that as long as governments have existed, the people and institutions running them have needed to collect information about potential uprisings and challenges to their authority. Informants were employed in ancient civilizations primarily for cases of treason. As suggested by Bloom (2002), rulers wished to maintain power and informers helped them achieve this goal. Ancient rulers were in constant fear that they would be overthrown and concerned about plots against them. This was illustrated in the history of Athens, where any person (regardless of station) could come forward and offer information regarding a treasonous act that had occurred or was going to occur. In 415 BCE, one well-known informant was Andocides (Marr, 1971). Andocides was born in 440 BCE to one of the most prominent Athenian families. He was an orator and politician who was frequently criticized for his political beliefs. In 415 BCE, he was named as a coconspirator with Alcibiades, who was accused of destroying sacred pillars called *Hermae*. This occurred on the eve of the day that the Athenian fleet was to set sail to Syracuse during the Peloponnesian War. The pillars were thought to ward off evil and protect the borders from harm, so toppling these statues was horribly impious. Androcides was seized and thrown into prison. To spare himself and avoid the death penalty, he informed on his coconspirators, one of whom was his father. As the saying goes, the apple does not fall far from the tree—Androcides's father also escaped the death penalty by providing the names of his accomplices (Marr, 1971).

In ancient Athens, treason was punishable by death, and informing on other treasonous parties would reduce one's sentence to banishment instead of execution. However, if the informant's information turned out to be untrue, the informant was put to death. Thus, for those who had already been convicted of treason, it would only make sense for them to become informants—regardless of the veracity of the information—because doing so increased their chances of survival. This is a common theme throughout the history of informant testimony. The penalty for fabricating evidence is no worse than the existing punishment the informant is facing. Therefore, there is no risk to fabricating information, only the potential for reward. After all, the death sentence can be carried out only once! In the parlance of betting, for someone sentenced to death the odds are in favor of manufacturing a good story because the outcome of being proved a liar is the same as not informing on another person—execution.

Middle Ages

English common law recognized both "approvers" and "common informers" (Rich, 2010). Approvers were convicted felons who provided testimony against their fellow accomplices or other criminals in exchange for a royal pardon (Rich, 2010). Common informers were citizens, not felons, who reported minor crimes and were rewarded with half of the assessed fine or half the value of the goods recovered.

The approver system dates as far back as 1275, and it was like the systems used in the ancient world in that approvers were expected to inform on others to gain their own freedom (Zimmerman, 1994). Approvers were required to admit guilt and then identify several of their accomplices. They could become approvers only if they had committed treason or another felony. Approvers were required to confess before the completion of the final evidence in the trial. There were several constraints on the approvers (Zimmerman, 1994). For instance, an accuser could not retract a confession and accuse another person of the crime. Even back in the thirteenth century, courts found approver testimony to be dubious, and once the testimony was heard the court could issue a cautionary instruction to the tribunal indicating that it was dangerous to convict solely based on the uncorroborated evidence of the approver.[1] Furthermore, the court could decide if the approver was even allowed to testify. The accused had two ways to respond to the accuser: take their chance at trial or choose combat—challenge the approver to a fight. If the accused was convicted, the accuser was free to go but had to leave the country. However, if there was no conviction the approver was executed (Zimmerman, 1994).

As should be obvious, there were many problems with the approver system, and as will become clear, several of these same issues still plague the judicial system today. Chief among these problems is that the courts were relying on criminals to tell the truth. These people had previously been arrested, confessed to breaking the law, and then had taken an oath to tell the truth. Zimmerman (1994) called into question the credibility of approvers, who would profit or even save their life by making an accusation. The credibility problem was exacerbated by the consequences of an acquittal, in which the approver would be executed. One would think that there could be no greater incentive to lie than to preserve one's own life (see Trott, 1996). However, the credibility of the approver and the corroboration of the testimony were not the only problems afflicting the approver system. There was also extortion—sheriffs and jailors would attempt to extort money from the innocent by compelling inmates to become approvers and accuse innocent people of various crimes. Despite these problems, the major benefit of the approver system was that the authorities were sometimes made aware of crimes they otherwise would not have discovered. According to Zimmerman (1994), the formal approver system was abandoned by the end of the medieval period, but many of the underlying characteristics of the modern informer system have roots in the approver system.

The Common Informer: The Tudor and Stuart Years

The "common informer" system in sixteenth-century England was like the medieval approver system. Under the common informer system, anyone could bring illegal actions to the attention of the authorities. Unlike under the approver system, if the prosecution of the accused was successful, the informant was entitled to half the value of the seized goods or half the fine, and the remaining half went to the Crown (Davies, 2017). According to Davies, however, informers to the court did not benefit too much in terms of money from the prosecution. For example, the Crown's most successful informer earned over the course of his career about twenty-two pounds (see Davies, 2017)—a few thousand dollars in today's currency. Despite this minimal compensation, informers endured and found ways to profit from the system, using both legal and illegal means.

A typical way for common informers to increase their profits was to avoid the judicial system altogether so that they would not have to split their profits with the Crown (Davies, 2017). Potential informers could extort money or goods from their target by promising not to become a Crown witness in exchange for some benefit or payment. According to Davies (2017), this extortion involved not only a promise to avoid the authorities but also preventing others from going to the authorities. In this way, informers served as a type of protection or insurance. For example, Griffin Flood (a known informant; see Anonymous, 1623) came to discover that a foreign man was working illegally. Instead of turning him in, he took a monthly fee to keep quiet and to deter other informants from reporting the foreigner. While informers like Flood were able to benefit financially, the Crown lost out on any revenue that would have been recovered from the conviction. Moreover, the crime could continue because the authorities were kept ignorant of any illegality.

Although the Crown did not always enjoy the monetary benefits that the informer system generated, it did work to protect informers from violence. This was important because informers were negatively perceived by the public and subject to attack. Take the informant Flood again (see Anonymous, 1623): he informed against a woman for employing a foreign tailor to mend some clothes as payment for his debt. The woman was successfully prosecuted, and Flood was paid for his service. However, the woman in question, in an act of retaliation, hit Flood in the head with a pewter pot, injuring him. When the authorities came, she claimed that Flood tried to take sexual advantage of her. Given Flood's poor reputation as an informer, he was convicted in court. Part of his sentence required him to pay the woman considerable compensation in addition to a jail term.

The Crown did not want retributive acts like the above to deter informants from being willing to inform on others. Therefore, the Crown delivered proclamations to protect informers from public sentiment and violence (see Davies, 2017), as evidenced by Elizabeth II's Proclamation 547, which protected those acting as informers from reprisal by forbidding common citizens from mistreating informers. The Crown believed that informers must not be hindered or discouraged from their actions because informants allowed for the administration of justice and helped to ensure a revenue stream from convicted felons. In this way the Crown acknowledged that informers provided a useful and beneficial service to both the Crown and society—so much so that the Crown felt that the system and its practitioners were worth protecting. The Crown, however, was aware of the problems with the informer system and tried to fix them by instituting proclamations such as a 1635 declaration from the court of Charles I (Davies, 2017), which aimed to prevent informers from committing frauds and abuses by holding them accountable.

Ultimately, the Crown benefitted from the informer system in three ways. First, the system generated at least some revenue because the Crown received half the bounty when the accused was convicted (see Davies, 2017). Second, the Crown learned about crimes and criminals that would have been undiscovered without the assistance of the informer system. Although one could argue that some of this information was garnered through manipulative intent and/or that these were ill-gotten gains, the Crown did not view it this way. Finally, at least in theory, the informer system acted as a deterrent to commit crime. The rationale for this was that people would be less likely to commit crimes because they would be worried that someone might inform on them. Criminals now had to worry about not just the police but their friends and neighbors as well. However, as was the case with Flood, the system may have fostered the creation of new crimes (such as extortion). The common informer system was by no means perfect. Still, the Crown did not abolish it; despite its flaws, it was viewed as better than no system at all.

Eighteenth-Century England: The Ryder Years

Much of the modern English and American judicial systems are derived from the judicial system of eighteenth-century England, and Langbein (1983) reports that well-known tenets of both the English and the American legal systems—the law of evidence, the adversarial system, the prohibition against self-incrimination, and the main rules for the relationship between the judge and the jury—emerged during this period. At this time the English court used the "Crown witness system," whose origins can be traced back to the medieval approver system. According to Langbein (1983), Crown witnesses were typically employed in gang cases or other cases in which there was more than one perpetrator. The witness would agree to admit their role in a crime and would give evidence against their coconspirators in exchange for leniency. In today's terms, Crown witnesses would be referred to as accomplice witnesses (see Natapoff, 2009). This period in the English judicial system laid the foundation for the modern-day informer system.[2]

In this section, we summarize Langbein's (1983) writings on the English court system as it relates to the development and history of informers. Before beginning, it is important to consider the sources that Langbein used. In the eighteenth century, court reporting was not what it is today. As a result, scholars like Langbein are forced to rely on a set of pamphlets that served as the record of the criminal proceedings at the Old Bailey—the trial court reserved for serious crimes committed in London and the adjacent county of Middlesex. It is also the central criminal court of England and Wales. The pamphlets from the Old Bailey are known as the Old Bailey Session Papers (OBSP). The OBSP supposedly recorded verbatim accounts of every trial at the court, including the verdict. The problem with these accounts for a legal historian, as stated by Langbein, is that the pamphlets were not meant to set legal precedent and are often incomplete. The most serious issues for historians might be what Langbein refers to as the editorial policy of the publisher, who attempted to embellish the proceedings to make the pamphlets more entertaining to the reading public. These embellishments make the documents of dubious quality for historians—especially since there is no way to verify their accuracy. Langbein, however, compared the OBSP to the notes of Sir Dudley Ryder, hence the title of this section. Ryder was a judge at the Old Bailey from 1754 until his death two years later. It was just as common then as it is now for judges to take notes during trials. Ryder was skilled in shorthand, so his notes are detailed and remain accessible. Most importantly, they allowed Langbein to verify the accounts in the OBSP for the forty-four trials over which Ryder presided.

For the remainder of this section, we summarize Langbein's (1983) findings about criminal trials and judicial law in the 1700s as related to the modern-day informer system. Langbein relied on many eighteenth-century English trials to illustrate his points about Crown witnesses and competition among them to testify before their coconspirators. As will be discussed later, it was important to be the first to cooperate with authorities, as latecomers were often unable to trade information for leniency. We will borrow some of his examples to continue to trace the history of the informant system.

As mentioned earlier, the Crown witness system involved culprits or accomplices granted immunity in exchange for admitting guilt and identifying their accomplices, generally in a gang. Langbein (1983) offered the case of Charles Cane as an illustrative example of the pros and cons of the system. In 1755, at around the age of eighteen, Cane became a Crown witness. He had been a member of a gang of robbers and was arrested for stealing cloaks, frocks, and other items from an unattended house. While the rest of the gang escaped, Cane and one of his accomplices stayed in the house and were promptly arrested when the authorities arrived. The stolen goods were later sold for less than three pounds by the accomplices, who escaped in what Langbein referred to as the "notorious Black Boy Alley" (p. 86). Black Boy Alley was a gang of criminals that operated in England in the eighteenth century (McMahon, 2019). It turned out that the police raiding party was not there on account of Cane and his gang but were there for an entirely different matter. Nevertheless, Cane thought the police were there because of his robbery and promptly asked if he could testify against his accomplices. Cane's request was accepted, and he appeared as a Crown witness. Interestingly, when Cane's accomplice Francis Preyer was captured, he also immediately requested to be a Crown witness, but police said they would admit him only if he could contribute more than what Cane had already provided. Preyer apparently had little additional information, as he and his accomplices were convicted and sentenced to death based on Cane's testimony. Cane walked free but committed additional crimes and was subsequently convicted of robbery two years later and sentenced to death. The evidence presented against him was the statement of one of his new gang members, who had become a Crown witness himself!

The above example of the informant Cane and his demise illustrates that there was no honor among Crown witnesses. There was, as there is today, great competition as to who could get to the police first to become a Crown witness. As we saw in both cases above involving Cane, all the gang members were willing to inform on one another to save their own necks. Regarding Cane's eventual conviction, his new gang was ready to compete against one another to offer evidence to the Crown to avoid conviction. According to Langbein (1983), it is unclear why or how, but there was a time when Cane was convicted for a non-capital offense because he had lost the competition to be the first informant. A man named Cole, the winner of the informant battle, testified that "the justice made me the evidence, because I was the first that confessed" (Langbein, 1983, p. 89). After his first conviction, Cane was immediately tried for another case of shoplifting in front of the same jury. Cole, once again, testified for the Crown against Cane—and once again Cane was convicted. Presumably, Cole was set free to commit more crimes and testify against other accomplices.

The cases described above highlight an inherent flaw (even in 1755) with the Crown witness system: once informants finished testifying in court against their fellow criminals, they were free (if the defendants were convicted) to return to the streets and commit more crimes. The former issue was noted in a quote that Langbein (1983) references: "These evidences [referring to Crown witnesses], as soon as their accomplices are convicted, and discharged, and with this addition of infamy, are turned into the streets to remain the contempt and terror of society. This sort of reception from the Public never fails to induce the unhappy criminal to endeavor to raise a fresh gang. . . . He soon finds proper associates; and there hardly passes a [session at the Old Bailey] when one or more are not convicted, who perhaps the preceding [sessions] were evidences" (Welch, 1753, quoted in Langbein, 1983, p. 85).

Another major issue with informant testimony noted by the eighteenth-century English court was corroboration. Often, no corroboration of an informant's testimony was required in court. Let us return to the Crown witness Cole. After helping to convict Cane, Cole still had several other hearings to attend at the Old Bailey to ensure that the rest of the Cane gang was imprisoned (see Langbein, 1983). Cole testified against Cane and three others. All the cases involved either the Cane gang members or individuals who had received their stolen goods. One of these hearings was for Richard Munday, who had worked with Cole shoplifting items. According to the Ryder papers, as reported by Langbein, Munday attempted to impeach Cole by saying that "he is a very great villain, he will say anything to save his own life." Munday's statement was likely accurate but ultimately not persuasive enough, as he was convicted of shoplifting because (at least in this one case) Cole's testimony was corroborated by an eyewitness.

To deal with the possibility that an informant would present false testimony without corroboration, the court put the Corroboration Rule (later termed the law of evidence) into effect. Essentially, the Corroboration Rule stated that supporting evidence must be presented in addition to accomplice testimony and that a conviction must not rest solely on the statements of an accomplice witness. The Corroboration Rule was subsequently called the Accomplice Rule. Cole's testimony against Munday and Munday's conviction despite his attempt to impeach Cole illustrated the need for a rule like this. Munday's argument, although not successful, raised a very important question: should juries take the word of criminals, especially those facing a death sentence, as the sole evidence against an accomplice? The Crown recognized this as a problem, but it was not until the end of the century that they started discouraging the practice of convicting on the sole basis of an accomplice's testimony.

The Accomplice Rule did not come without its critics, however. Henry Fielding, an English magistrate (and a well-known novelist), believed that this rule hindered his ability to obtain a conviction. His primary argument was that all cases should be presented to a jury, regardless of the strength of the evidence (or lack thereof). The English courts eventually gave Fielding what he wanted. In *R. v. Atwood and Robbins* (1788), a jury could convict based on uncorroborated accomplice testimony, but accomplices were to be brought to the triers of fact. It was now the duty of the judge to caution jurors against the inherent unreliable nature of accomplice witness testimony, but ultimately it was the jury's responsibility to ascertain the credibility of witnesses.

Another product of the Crown witness system was its relationship to the creation of one of the earliest forms of the confession rule (Langbein, 1983). This rule argued that a pretrial confession that was "free and voluntary" warranted more credit compared to a confession that was not (i.e., resulting from torture or fear). This rule is based on the idea that if a confession is not free and voluntary it warrants no credit (Leach at 263–64, 168 Eng. Rep. at 235, K.B. 1783). As noted by Wigmore (1908), the confession rule foreshadowed the Anglo-American law of evidence that included "exclusionary rules" (Langbein, 1983). Exclusionary rules prevent evidence that was collected illegally from being used at trial. Some legal experts estimate that the confession rule emerged from the period of 1775 to 1785 (Wigmore, 1908). Wigmore describes the courts as having "a general suspicion of all confessions, a prejudice against them as such, and an inclination to repudiate them upon the slightest pretext." To understand this caution toward confessions, Wigmore conjectured that judges were possibly concerned that social status was at play, with the poor bending to the will of the socially superior.

In summary, the main purpose in becoming a Crown witness was avoiding prosecution. But until the final quarter of the eighteenth century, there was no statute or law that prevented authorities from reneging on their offers. Instead, Langbein (1983) suggested it was fear that kept constables and the Crown true to their promises. In other words, if the Crown prosecuted informers after they testified, word would spread and criminals would no longer come forward to give evidence against their accomplices. If there was no benefit to the witness, why would any criminal present evidence?

The Beginning of the Modern-Day Jailhouse Informer

In the early years of the modern informer system, the police departments in both France and England became much more organized and effective. In France, Eugène-François Vidocq is credited with establishing a network of informers to help combat crime (Ashley, 2015; Conliffe, 2019). When Vidocq was a young man, he caught the woman he fell in love with cheating on him with a solider. Vidocq savagely beat the soldier and was jailed for the attack. After several escapes and recaptures, Vidocq decided to turn his life around and live on the straight and narrow.[3] But after he was arrested for fencing stolen goods, he offered his services to the police as an informant. His offer was accepted, and he went to prison and began providing the police with information about criminal activities in France. After twenty-one months, Vidocq was rewarded for his efforts with his release. Vidocq continued to use his contacts and knowledge of the criminal world to report criminal activities. Soon thereafter, Vidocq was appointed to lead the criminal investigation unit in Paris known as the Paris Sûreté, and during this time he set up a network of informers (Conliffe, 2019).

In England in 1877, a barrister named Howard Vincent followed the lead of Vidocq and created the Criminal Investigation Department (CID). As part of his duties, he went to France to observe the French police system (Bloom, 2005). Vincent was so impressed with what he saw that he came back to England and set up the CID with himself as the head. Like Vidocq in France, the CID also created a network of informers.

The United States, too, developed informer systems in the nineteenth century. The first documented jailhouse informant case in America occurred in Manchester, Vermont, in 1819 (Warden, 2004). Two brothers, Jesse and Stephen Boorn, were accused of killing their brother-in-law, Russell Colvin. The Boorn brothers had made no secret of their distaste for Colvin, and when Colvin went missing, suspicion fell upon the brothers. Jesse Boorn shared a cell with Silas Merill, a known and convicted forger. Merill testified that Jesse confessed to him about the brothers killing Colvin. Based on Merill's testimony, Jesse and Stephen were sentenced to death. In an unusual twist of fate, however, the brothers were not executed. Instead, Merill's testimony was shown to be false, as Colvin turned up alive in New Jersey.

Jailhouse Informants in the Contemporary US Courtroom

In the two hundred years since the first jailhouse informants appeared in a US courtroom, we have seen three important historical trends. First, in prior eras individuals were not detained in jails to the same degree as in the modern era (US Bureau of Justice Statistics, 1984, 2020), hence the current jailhouse informant phenomenon is unique to modern American mass incarceration. Second, in the modern era jailhouse informants testify in a variety of cases. However, the proliferation of jailhouse informant testimony during this time led to the uncovering of many instances of false jailhouse informant testimony, sometimes due to illegal behavior by the government. The initial uncovering of misconduct was not the result of a government inquiry but was instead due to several articles in the *Los Angeles Times* in late 1988 and early 1989 about jailhouse informant Leslie Vernon White (Rohrlich, 1988a, 1988b, 1989; see also chapter 6). White then appeared on the television show *60 Minutes* in February 1989 to explain how he fabricated testimony. Although White was not the only prolific jailhouse informant to receive attention for his perjured testimony, he is notable because his interview was aired on national television and seen by millions of viewers. White was well acquainted with the California judicial system; he had been in and out of jail since the age of eight. In his nationally televised interview, he described the methods that he used to obtain the information needed for him to testify as a jailhouse informant. For example, to gain information from an inmate, White would sometimes deliberately have his own cell moved so that he could have access to that inmate. But White did not need to have access to an inmate to secure information about that inmate's case. White would obtain the correct factual profile of a case, including information that would be known only to the perpetrator, by calling official offices (e.g., police department, coroner's office, district attorney's office, etc.) and posing as a police officer; he would simply ask law enforcement officials for the information, all from a pay phone in the prison. Still posing as a police officer, he would then arrange to be transported with a specific defendant to court, so he could document that he and the defendant had the opportunity to talk. Armed with a false secondary confession that matched the fact pattern of the case and having arranged to be near the suspect, White would then trade his testimony for his freedom. At trial, White was a believable witness because he provided information that only the true perpetrator would have known. For this compelling testimony, he received incentives including early release from jail and monetary compensation (Bloom, 2002).

The articles and the *60 Minutes* interview prompted legal groups in California to call for a grand jury to investigate the use and mechanisms of informant witnesses. The subsequent report of the Los Angeles County Grand Jury (1990) depicted the use of jailhouse informants over a ten-year period (1979–1989). The report is thirty years old but still the most extensive report to date on the use of jailhouse informant testimony. The report outlined the use of jailhouse informants in 233 murder and other felony cases. The cases involved 120 witnesses, 147 exhibits, and thousands of documents, including court transcripts, internal memos, and district attorney files. The Grand Jury also interviewed many current and former jailhouse informants. It found that they were typically individuals who (a) were facing a lengthy prison sentence, (b) tended to reoffend, (c) were highly motivated to curry favor with the authorities, (d) were not committed to the truth, (e) were interested in serving their own interests, (f) had previously testified for the prosecution, and (g) desired a reward or benefit in exchange for their testimony or cooperation. The Grand Jury estimated that there were eighty to ninety jailhouse informants in Los Angeles County jail at any given time.

Overall, the report of the Los Angeles County Grand Jury (1990) exposed a culture of utilizing and rewarding inmates who provided incriminating information, often fabricated, about other inmates' reported confessions. The report noted that there were too many examples of perjury by jailhouse informants for the commission to reasonably count. Furthermore, the Los Angeles County Sheriff's Department was complicit in placing high-profile suspects in cells with jailhouse informants to procure evidence against the accused. For example, the report listed about twenty cases in which police actively took part in assisting jailhouse informants to collect information from other inmates. In each of these cases, inmates or jailhouse informants had their cells deliberately moved so they could have access to an inmate. In return for their help, jailhouse informants were given elevated status in jail, along with other benefits (e.g., extra visits, phone calls, access to television or movies, being moved to more desirable cells, even small amounts of money for the prison store). One informant testified that in exchange for his testimony, he received several thousand dollars, free rent, and living expenses when released from jail. Another informant testified that he received three hundred dollars for his testimony and that his wife was paid nine hundred dollars for his help in another case. A third jailhouse informant received rent for seven months. Many informants testified that they received the ultimate prize—freedom.

Despite the problems uncovered by the report of the Los Angeles County Grand Jury (1990), it did not recommend that the use of the jailhouse informants be banned. However, the report did suggest some reforms. First, the District Attorney's Office should keep a record of all jailhouse informants regarding the number of times they had testified in the past and what benefits they had received. Second, a complete record of all benefits to jailhouse informants should be maintained and all benefits should be disclosed to the defense prior to trial. In other words, there should be a record of implied promises of future benefits to come after the jailhouse informant's testimony. Third, the report stated that it was the duty of the prosecution to check the credibility of each jailhouse informant. Finally, the report recommended that the Los Angeles District Attorney's Office should establish a set of rules to disclose any benefits to the defense.

Another scandal involving jailhouse informants surfaced in 2011 and also involved negligence by the District Attorney's Office. In that year, seven people were killed by Scott Dekraai in the deadliest mass shooting in the history of Orange County, California. Dekraai's guilt aside, his trial would bring about a national scandal involving Orange County's District Attorney's Office and Sheriff's Department (Queally, 2019). Dekraai's defense lawyer, Scott Sanders, accused sheriff's deputies of placing Fernando Perez, a well-known informant who had previously informed on another of Sanders's clients, next to Dekraai's cell. This accusation launched a federal investigation, resulting in the disqualification by Orange County Supreme Court judge Thomas Goethals of any lawyer (about 250 of them) involved with the District Attorney's Office from prosecuting Dekraai (Laird, 2016).

During his own investigation, Sanders discovered potentially thousands of documents that were never disclosed to the defense—a serious violation of civil rights (see chapter 2). Along with his over five-hundred-page motion, Sanders submitted fifteen thousand pages as exhibits. One piece of evidence Sanders uncovered was Tred, an online database tracking the use of jailhouse informants that had been maintained by the Orange County Sheriff's Department (Laird, 2016). Tred contained the reasons for inmate movements and records of jailhouse informant work. It should be noted that Tred was not a new program—it had been installed on computers since the 1990s (Laird, 2016). Although Orange County District Attorney Todd Spitzer had enacted policies stating that his approval must be obtained before using jailhouse informants at trial, no serious action was taken against his office or the sheriff's department. It should be noted that Dekraii, the defendant in this case, pleaded guilty to the mass killing in 2017 (Saavedra, 2017).

The third important historical trend of the past two hundred years is that legal action (both rules of evidence and court decisions) has continued to allow jailhouse informants to testify in the courtroom. These actions will be described in detail later, but we briefly note the following six critical actions:

1. Jailhouse informant testimony is not hearsay testimony and thus is allowed in court (Michigan Legal Publishing, 2019)
2. Jailhouse informant testimony does not constitute illegal search and seizure (*Hoffa v. US*, 1966)
3. Protections against self-incrimination do not apply when a defendant speaks to a jailhouse informant (*Illinois v. Perkins*, 1990)
4. Despite earlier rulings to the contrary (e.g., *Massiah v. US*, 1964), it is now legal for a jailhouse informant to obtain information from a defendant without counsel for the defense being present (*Kuhlmann v. Wilson*, 1986)
5. Incentives given to jailhouse informants do not constitute bribery (*US v. Singleton*, 1999)
6. All incentives offered to a jailhouse informant must be turned over to the defense as part of the case evidence (*Brady v. Maryland*, 1963; *Giglio v. US*, 1972)

We should note that despite legal actions tending to favor prosecutors' use of jailhouse informants, in the past five years several states have enacted laws to regulate the use of jailhouse informant testimony. For example, Connecticut enacted a law in 2019 (S.B. 1098, 2019) that protects the accused from jailhouse informant testimony. This law was inspired by the wrongful conviction of Alfred Swinton, who, as we saw earlier, served eighteen years of a sixty-year sentence before being exonerated by DNA evidence. One of the major pieces of evidence against Swinton was the testimony of a jailhouse informant who testified that Swinton confessed that he had sex with and killed the victim (Backus, 2019). This law requires that at the defense's request, the prosecutors must disclose their intent to use a jailhouse informant and the substance of the testimony. The prosecution must disclose any benefit that has been promised to the jailhouse informant, and the defense is entitled to a pretrial reliability hearing regarding the testimony. Finally, the law established the first statewide tracking system for jailhouse informants, to include any jailhouse informant witness testimony and any benefits that have or will be provided/offered.

Similar jailhouse informant testimony laws have been enacted in other states, such as Florida (enacted in 2019; Fla. R. Crim. P. 3.220, 2019), Illinois (enacted in 2018; IL S.B. 1830, 2018), Nebraska (enacted in 2019; Nebraska Revised Statute 29-4704, 2019), Oklahoma (enacted in 2020; OK SB 1385, 2020), and Texas (enacted in 2017; H.B. 34, 2017). In 2019, Florida adopted a rule of criminal procedure requiring that when using jailhouse informants, prosecutors must disclose the substance and circumstances of the jailhouse informant's statements, the informant's complete criminal history, and other cases in which the informant cooperated with law enforcement in exchange for benefits. Illinois now requires judges to hold pretrial reliability hearings before jailhouse informant testimony is admissible in murder, sexual assault, and arson cases. Prosecutors must also disclose any benefits provided in exchange for jailhouse informant testimony and any previous informant activities. Similar information is also required when using jailhouse informants in Oklahoma and Nebraska. Texas requires the establishment of a system to track the use of jailhouse informants and any benefits offered in exchange for their testimony and to disclose specific impeaching information to the defense.

Summary

Throughout this chapter we have shown that there are clear themes related to the use of informants that seem to reoccur. From ancient times to the present, the government, or those in power, have noted a benefit to using informants. More specifically, governments have felt that informants provide authorities with knowledge about crimes that would otherwise go unsolved or undetected (Roth, 2016). However, this benefit has come with a cost that ancient, medieval, and modern courts have all recognized—how credible and reliable is the word of those who have already (or potentially) broken the law and who are giving evidence to lessen or eliminate their own punishment? As early as the eighteenth century, the English court attempted to deal with this issue with the establishment of the Corroboration Rule. Modern courts are still struggling with this issue, as evidenced by the new laws in several states. We will next review the legal status of jailhouse informant testimony and the various legal opinions and court decisions about jailhouse informants in the United States.

2

Legal Perspectives on Admitting Jailhouse Informant Testimony

In the Nassau County, New York, courthouse on November 6, 1986, Stephen Dorfman took the witness stand, promising to tell the truth, the whole truth, and nothing but the truth. Dorfman testified that he had heard John Restivo, the defendant, confess to the rape and murder of a young girl. Considered the prosecution's star witness, Dorfman had a long criminal history and had been offered to have his seven- to fourteen-year sentence reduced to four to eight years for testifying. Dorfman's testimony was critical to the case because the prosecution had been able to present only circumstantial evidence. The prosecution's gamble paid off, and despite his adamant claims of innocence, Restivo was convicted of rape and murder and sentenced to thirty-three and a half years to life. Later, it was determined that the jurors had convicted the wrong man. New DNA evidence conclusively proved that Restivo could not have been the perpetrator, and on December 29, 2005, Restivo was exonerated, having served eighteen years in jail for a murder he never committed. Clearly, Dorfman had perjured himself on the stand, knowingly costing an innocent man nearly two decades of his life to procure a better outcome for himself (*People v. Restivo*, 1986).

Notwithstanding that Dorfman's testimony led to a false conviction, the case highlights that the use of jailhouse informant testimony both is legal and occurs on a regular basis. Jailhouse informant testimony adheres to the Federal Rules of Evidence (Michigan Legal Publishing, 2019) and is allowed in most states. In addition, the circumstances of a jailhouse informant receiving information from a defendant have generally been ruled not to violate a specific federal law (e.g., the bribery statute) nor to impact a defendant's constitutional rights. In this chapter, we review both the rules of evidence that allow jailhouse informant testimony and specific US court rulings that have been critical in shaping the use of jailhouse informants (primarily) by prosecutors.

Rules of Evidence: Jailhouse Informant Testimony Is Not Hearsay

At first glance, jailhouse informant testimony might appear to involve hearsay because an informant hears details about a crime from another person. Keep in mind that hearsay is defined as a statement (not made under oath) that (a) the declarant does not make while testifying at the current trial or hearing and (b) a party offers in evidence to prove the truth of the matter asserted in the statement (Michigan Legal Publishing, 2019). If hearsay, jailhouse informant testimony would be prohibited in most criminal trials by the Federal Rules of Evidence. This prohibition is based on the way that hearsay (not involving a jailhouse informant) (a) may make cross-examination of the original declarant difficult (Wigmore, 1970), (b) compromises the Sixth Amendment right of the defendant to face witnesses testifying against them (Colb, 2008), and (c) may be valued too highly by jurors because the declarant's statement cannot be properly scrutinized through cross-examination of the declarant (Sevier, 2015). We should note that despite the prohibition against hearsay testimony, there are over twenty exceptions when hearsay testimony can be allowed in court. For example, the "excited utterance" exception permits hearsay testimony if the statement recounted was made by a speaker under the "stress of excitement" caused by a startling event or condition (Michigan Legal Publishing, 2019). The basis for the excited utterance exception is spontaneity and close emotional proximity to the event in question, with the theory being that the event produces a condition of excitement in which an utterance is made that does not involve fabrication (Michigan Legal Publishing, 2019).

Despite jailhouse informant testimony appearing to meet certain criteria of hearsay testimony, it is typically *not* considered hearsay according to definitions provided by the Federal Rules of Evidence, Rule 801 (Michigan Legal Publishing, 2019). The Federal Rules of Evidence make clear that hearsay does *not* include "opposing party's statements," such as when defendants (an opposing party) make a statement against themselves (e.g., admitting that they committed a crime; Smith, 2013). Such a statement would include admitting their role in a specific crime to another person (i.e., a jailhouse informant). It is assumed that individuals will not admit or make statements against their interest unless said statements are in fact true.

Two important points should be noted about opponent-party statements. First, because opponent-party statements are not considered hearsay exceptions, there are no guarantees of trustworthiness as in the case of the other exceptions (Federal Rules of Evidence Advisory Committee notes as cited in Edwards, 2013). That is, hearsay exceptions are allowed in court because it is assumed that in unique circumstances it allows for some degree of truth. Going back to the excited utterance exception, it is assumed that a child who was sexually assaulted would not blurt out what happened to them out of the blue unless the law maintains some belief that the assault occurred and therefore would allow hearsay testimony. With opponent-party statements there are no such assumptions because the statements are not considered hearsay. Instead, they are presented by a jailhouse informant like other statements made during trial, and there is no assumption of truth.

Second, related to the point above, because opponent-party statements concern a party's own statements, a policy of fairness permits these statements to be used by the prosecution (see Edwards, 2013). That is, admitting these statements is "the result of the adversary system rather than satisfaction of the conditions of the hearsay rule" (Federal Rules of Evidence Advisory Committee notes as cited in Edwards, 2013). In this way, Edwards (2013) notes that the Federal Rules of Evidence endorse a "generous treatment of this avenue to admissibility" (Federal Rules of Evidence Advisory Committee notes as cited in Edwards, 2013). They also assume that the party who made the statements to another person (including a jailhouse informant) can defend these statements while on the stand. Of course, taking the stand is the last thing most defendants want to do during a trial because doing so opens the door to a wide variety of questioning during cross-examination by the prosecution.

While it is clear that jailhouse informant testimony can be presented as evidence in court, legal questions have arisen over the past sixty years concerning whether various aspects of jailhouse informant testimony are illegal based on a particular federal law or if it violates a defendant's constitutional rights. These questions concern the nature of the communication between a jailhouse informant and a defendant, the right of a defendant to counsel, the use of incentives with jailhouse informants, and the sharing of information supplied by a jailhouse informant. We discuss these questions in turn.

Question 1: Does the Fourth Amendment prohibit a jailhouse informant from obtaining information from a defendant if the informant does not announce working with the prosecution because it involves an illegal search and seizure of evidence?

In the mid-1960s union president Jimmy Hoffa and his associates argued that an illegal search and seizure of evidence occurred when they were brought to trial in a federal court on charges of bribing jurors in an earlier trial against Hoffa. After the earlier trial, the government obtained evidence from an informant that Hoffa and others had bribed the jurors in the earlier trial. As an incentive, the informant received payments from the federal government (i.e., a permissible incentive), and unrelated state and federal charges against the informant were either dropped or not actively pursued. Hoffa and his associates were convicted of bribery in this second case.

Hoffa appealed his conviction by arguing that his Fourth Amendment rights were violated because the informer failed to disclose his connection to the government, thereby violating any consent Hoffa had given for the informant's presence at the locations where conversations took place. In essence, Hoffa argued that the informant was conducting an illegal search. However, the US Supreme Court ruled against Hoffa (*Hoffa v. US*, 1966) and argued that the informant's presence did not constitute an illegal search, given that the informant was an invited guest. Moreover, the Court stated that Hoffa was relying upon misplaced confidence that the informer would not testify to what Hoffa had said. We will return to the *Hoffa v. US* case again when discussing safeguards against unreliable testimony because the ruling in this case specifically addressed the ability of jurors to distinguish informants' true and false testimony.

The *Hoffa v. US* (1966) ruling was extended in a later ruling involving the use of technology to obtain information from a defendant. In this later case, *US v. White* (1971), the defendant (James White) was tried for drug offenses. White and an informant (Harvey Jackson) had met in the latter's home and in other locations, and their conversations were electronically recorded. During the trial, the informant could not be located and thus did not testify. Instead, government agents who had listened to the recordings testified about conversations between the defendant and the informant. The defense argued that the testimony of the government agents should not be allowed because (a) the conversations were recorded without White's permission, (b) White had a reasonable expectation of privacy, and (c) the conversations were recorded without a warrant (i.e., violation of Fourth Amendment rights against unreasonable search and seizure). The US Supreme Court, as in the *Hoffa v. US* (1966) ruling, did not bar the agents' testimony and permitted them to describe the electronically recorded conversations.

Question 2: Does the Fifth Amendment prohibit a jailhouse informant from obtaining information from a defendant because the latter is protected against self-incrimination?

Although the Fifth Amendment protects a defendant against being compelled to self-incriminate, the US Supreme Court ruled that when a defendant speaks to a jailhouse informant, protections against self-incrimination do not apply. In *Illinois v. Perkins* (1990), an undercover police officer (John Parisi) was placed in jail with the defendant (Lloyd

Perkins) prior to the latter being charged with murder. This informant / police officer was able to elicit incriminating statements from Perkins. However, the defense argued that a Miranda warning (*Miranda v. Arizona*, 1966) was required when the jailhouse informant asked questions that could elicit an incriminating result.

Despite the defense's claim, the US Supreme Court ruled that self-incrimination is not implicated when defendants are unaware that they are speaking to law enforcement. Moreover, the Court stated that a jail context did not constitute an official interrogation (i.e., not a "police-dominated atmosphere") where compulsion to confess is present. Thus, the Court ruled that any statements made by the defendant were motivated only by his desire to impress his fellow inmate. The Court also argued that the defendant had no reason to think that the police agent had legal authority to force the defendant to give testimony, and in such a situation the defendant showed no signs of being intimidated.

The *Illinois v. Perkins* (1990) ruling was a setback for defendants' rights involving making incriminating statements, but another US Supreme Court ruling did offer some Fifth Amendment protections. In this case (*Arizona v. Fulminante*, 1991), the defendant Oreste Fulminante confessed to a fellow inmate (Anthony Sarivola) that he committed a murder, in exchange for protection from other inmates that Sarivola would provide. The Arizona State Supreme Court held that Fulminante's confession was coerced because he was motivated to confess only by fear of physical violence from the other inmates; the case had to be retried. This ruling was upheld by the US Supreme Court, which added that a coerced confession (a) runs the risk of being unreliable and (b) has a major impact on a jury.

Question 3: Does the Sixth Amendment prohibit a jailhouse informant from obtaining information from a defendant without counsel for the defense being present?

The fundamental guarantee of the Sixth Amendment is the right to have the assistance of counsel. This right is critical because it allows for equality between the defense and the state during the judicial process. Over the years, several court cases have examined whether the use of jailhouse informants interferes with this right to counsel. We will examine five critical US Supreme Court rulings on this issue. Some of these cases specifically involve jailhouse informants, while others involve other types of informants, but they all impact the interaction between a jailhouse informant and a defendant. As we will see, while early cases resulted in the US Supreme Court supporting a defendant's right to counsel, the Court reversed itself in more recent cases, thereby harming a defendant's Sixth Amendment rights.

Massiah v. US (1964)

Winston Massiah was indicted on federal narcotics charges. He retained a lawyer and pleaded not guilty. While out on bail, Massiah talked to one of his codefendants (a government informer) in the absence of counsel. Their conversation was transmitted to a federal agent, who testified about the nature of the conversation during Massiah's trial. After Massiah's conviction, his defense argued that the government deliberately elicited the statements from Massiah after his indictment and in the absence of his counsel. The US Supreme Court upheld this argument and created a two-part test for detecting whether the right to counsel was violated in interrogation settings (*Massiah v. US*, 1964): (a) the person to whom the defendant spoke was a government agent and (b) the person to whom the defendant spoke "deliberately elicited" incriminating information from the defendant in the absence of counsel. The second part of this test is important to later cases.

Brewer v. Williams (1977)

More than a decade after *Massiah v. US* (1964), this second case went further in defining what constitutes deliberate elicitation in the context of one's claim to the Sixth Amendment right to counsel (*Brewer v.*

Williams, 1977). The case involved Robert Williams, who was charged with the murder of a ten-year-old girl in Des Moines, Iowa. Williams had a history of mental illness. After being arrested in Davenport, Iowa (160 miles away), two police detectives drove Williams back to Des Moines, a three-hour drive. Williams's attorney told him before the drive that the detectives were simply transporting him and that Williams should not speak with them at all about the alleged crime until arriving in Des Moines. However, the detectives talked to Williams during the drive and attempted to elicit information about the case. The detectives' attempt included using their knowledge that Williams was deeply religious to suggest that he should help them find the victim's body to give her a proper Christian burial. Ultimately, Williams led the detectives to the victim's body. At trial, Williams was convicted of murder. The defense appealed his conviction based on there being no counsel present during the questioning of Williams. The US Supreme Court agreed with the defense's argument and reversed Williams's conviction.

US v. Henry (1980)

The first two cases described above involved the elicitation of information outside of a jail context and did not involve jailhouse informants. However, the right to counsel for an incarcerated defendant raises other issues related to a jail context. For example, a defendant in jail has a strong desire to connect with other inmates, and incarceration includes unique daily pressures (Merritt, 2003). Both factors make it difficult to determine exactly when and why information has been elicited from a defendant. In *US v. Henry* (1980), defendant Billy Gale Henry was indicted for armed robbery of a bank. While Henry was in jail pending trial, the government contacted an inmate confined in the same cellblock as Henry. The inmate was told to be alert to any statements Henry made but not to specifically initiate a conversation with him regarding the bank robbery charge. Once released from jail, the jailhouse informant reported to a government agent that he and Henry had engaged in a conversation in which Henry incriminated himself in the bank robbery. The jailhouse informant was paid for this information, and Henry was convicted of the robbery. Henry appealed, arguing that his statements to the jailhouse informant should not have been admitted at trial because the government intentionally created a situation likely to cause him to make incriminating statements without the assistance of counsel. Henry argued that he was unaware that the jailhouse informant was acting for the government and thus could not be viewed as having waived his right to the assistance of counsel.

The US Supreme Court agreed with arguments raised by Henry and overturned the conviction. The Court found that the government had deliberately elicited incriminating statements in violation of the Sixth Amendment as interpreted under *Massiah v. US* (1964): (a) the informant was acting under government instructions on a contingency-fee basis, (b) the defendant was unaware that the informant was any more than a fellow inmate and thus would confide information inappropriate to give to an adversary, and (c) the defendant was incarcerated at the time of the conversation, imposing pressure on the defendant (Goodell, 2003). In making this ruling, the US Supreme Court acknowledged that deliberately eliciting information from a defendant could occur in jail as well as out of jail and that a jailhouse informant did not have to actively elicit information to violate a defendant's rights. The government in the *Henry* case must have known that some sort of elicitation of information would take place and that this could occur in various subtle ways. Moreover, by placing the jailhouse informant in Henry's cell to begin with, the government took steps to deliberately elicit statements from Henry.

Maine v. Moulton (1985)

About five years after the *US v. Henry* (1980) ruling, the US Supreme Court ruled in *Maine v. Moulton* (1985). As in the first two cases, this case did not involve a jailhouse informant but nevertheless offered important pronouncements about eliciting information without counsel present.

Goodell (2003) noted that *Maine v. Moulton* is often viewed as more consequential than *US v. Henry*, not because of the impact of the ruling but because later rulings involving the right to counsel seem to have forgotten the *Maine v. Moulton* case even existed. This case involved two defendants, Perley Moulton and Gary Colson, who were indicted on charges of burglary and theft. After being arrested, they were released on bail pending trial. The prosecution received a quick confession from Colson for his part in the crimes and offered him a deal of no further charges if he helped prosecute Moulton. Colson agreed and allowed his phone calls to be monitored and to wear an electronic monitor when he met with Moulton. During one meeting with Colson, Moulton incriminated himself. This secondary confession was presented at trial, where Moulton was convicted. An appeal to the Supreme Judicial Court of Maine was successful (a new trial was called for) because it was argued that Moulton's right to counsel when meeting with Colson was violated as Colson was working as an agent of the government.

The US Supreme Court upheld the Maine court's decision. The former argued that the police (i.e., the government) had interfered with Moulton's right to have an attorney present during the interaction between Moulton and Colson and that the government had to have known that Moulton would reveal information to Colson, given that the latter was known by Moulton to have been only his codefendant, not an agent of the government. In fact, if Moulton had known Colson was a government informant, the Court stated, it was unlikely that Moulton would have confessed. Based on these arguments, the Court acknowledged that the government has an obligation (an affirmative duty) not to act in a way that interferes with a defendant's right to counsel. Goodell (2003, p. 2529) noted that the Moulton case "seemed to go a step further than the Henry Court when it imputed to prosecutors an affirmative duty to respect an accused's Sixth Amendment rights."

Kuhlmann v. Wilson (1986)

The *US v. Henry* (1980) and *Maine v. Moulton* (1985) rulings appeared to narrow the ability of the government to use informants (even when an informant was acting passively) because their use violated the right to counsel afforded by the Sixth Amendment. The final case we discuss, which guides the use of jailhouse informants today, is *Kuhlmann v. Wilson* (1986). This case essentially reversed the thinking used to decide all prior Sixth Amendment cases involving informants, jailhouse or otherwise. This reversal might seem odd, given that *Kuhlmann v. Wilson* was decided only a short time after the *Moulton* case. *Kuhlmann v. Wilson* involved a robbery and murder in New York state. The defendant, Joseph Allan Wilson, was confined in a cell with a prisoner, Benny Lee, who had previously agreed to act as a passive jailhouse informant. Wilson made unsolicited incriminating statements, which Lee reported to police. A jury convicted Wilson of murder, but he appealed the case by arguing that his right to counsel was violated.

Despite all the other rulings described above that supported a defendant's Sixth Amendment rights to have counsel present during interactions between a defendant and an informant, the US Supreme Court ruled against Wilson (*Kuhlmann v. Wilson*, 1986). The Court argued that because the jailhouse informant Lee had not actively engaged Wilson in conversation about the crimes, Lee's actions could not be considered an interrogation. The Court held that a defendant, in claiming his right to counsel was violated, was required to show that the government and the jailhouse informant took some action, beyond merely listening, that was designed to deliberately elicit the defendant's remarks. However, Wilson did not show that this occurred.

The dissenting justices in *Kuhlmann v. Wilson* (1986) forcefully argued that the facts in this case were almost identical to those in *US v. Henry* (1980) and thus constituted a violation of the right to counsel. They argued that the informants in both cases received compensation for information, were told not to question the accused, and had engaged in conversations with the defendant that encouraged discussion of crimes. It also appeared that the jailhouse informants in both cases were able to develop some level of close rapport with the defendants such that incriminating information was revealed (Lappen, 1987). Discussing more than just the similarity in cases, the dissenting justices argued that it was not enough to apply a "deliberate-elicitation" standard that focused on the informant himself but that consideration of the entire course of government behavior should have been noted. The dissenters argued that the issue was whether the government's action had a "sufficient nexus" with an accused's admission of guilt and argued that most jailhouse informants are not truly "passive," given that jailhouse informants work with government agents.

That so many jailhouse informants collaborate with the government raises another legal issue related to the dissent in *Kuhlmann v. Wilson* (1986). Specifically, government agents often actively and deliberately place a jailhouse informant near the accused (i.e., targeting) in hopes of obtaining information from a defendant (Toinkovicz, 1988). Typically, a jailhouse informant is aware of the targeting, but it should be noted that targeting is distinct from an agreement between a jailhouse informant and the government (Goodell, 2003). In fact, the state can target a defendant without any agreement with a jailhouse informant. For example, the government may place a jailhouse informant who is talkative near a defendant, but not tell the informant anything about why this took place. Even in this situation, the mere fact that targeting of a defendant occurred would be deemed sufficient to show that the government is responsible for the informant's questioning and thus had violated the defendant's right to counsel (Goodell, 2003).

Despite the strong dissent in *Kuhlmann v. Wilson* (1986), the majority ruling in this case opened the floodgates regarding jailhouse informant testimony being allowed in the courtroom. If jailhouse informants can claim (and they are always able to do so) that they did not actively elicit information from a defendant, such testimony will likely be allowed as evidence. Of course the defendant can claim to not have divulged case information (let alone talked to the jailhouse informant) or can say (true or not) that any statements made to the jailhouse informant were in jest, but such denials may not be believed by a jury. Additionally, in another blow to defendants' ability to defend themselves from jailhouse informant testimony, there is no clear-cut method a judge can use to determine whether the jailhouse informant was active or passive in the receipt of information from the defendant. It is possible that there could be a recording of an interaction between a jailhouse informant and a defendant to make this determination, but such recordings are uncommon.

Question 4: Does a federal law (i.e., the Federal Bribery Statute) prohibit offering incentives to a jailhouse informant in exchange for testimony?

Jailhouse informants can and do approach the government on their own, with information already gathered from a defendant (e.g., the jailhouse informant Leslie Vernon). This information may be offered out of a sense of moral duty, but it is much more likely that a jailhouse informant (as discussed in the two previous chapters) is willing to disclose information about a defendant to get something in return—an incentive. This system of cooperation through incentives benefits both the prosecution and jailhouse informants. Incentives allow the prosecution to obtain critical evidence that may be otherwise inaccessible through the collection of other types of evidence (especially physical evidence, such as DNA). Evidence from a jailhouse informant may be the only way to convict a dangerous criminal through a trial or at least to persuade a guilty defendant to accept a plea bargain. At the same time, incentives benefit jailhouse informants by allowing them to receive something as a reward for their time and effort. These incentives vary but might include leniency in sentencing or (as noted in chapter 1) some other benefit (like jail privileges). Some have argued that the use of incentives allows for the effectiveness of the criminal justice system (Natapoff, 2009)—without jailhouse informants, many crimes would not be prosecuted.

In discussing incentives, it is important to note that federal court decisions have determined that incentivizing prosecution witnesses is legal in almost all cases and does not constitute bribery (i.e., offering something of value in return for testimony). However, the ultimate path to this determination was indirect. Two court decisions, known as *Singleton I* (*US v. Singleton*, 1998) and *Singleton II* (*US v. Singleton*, 1999), paved the way for allowing incentivized testimony including that of jailhouse informants (see also Fessinger et al., 2020). Sonya Singleton was convicted of money laundering and conspiracy to distribute cocaine. An important piece of evidence against her was testimony from Napoleon Douglas, previously convicted as a coconspirator and serving his sentence in another state. In exchange for Douglas's testimony, the government attorneys promised Douglas that they would not prosecute him for other offenses and that they would notify the sentencing judge and his parole board in his current state of his willingness to cooperate. For his cooperation in the Singleton trial, Douglas's sentence was reduced from fifteen years to five years.

On appeal, Singleton's lawyer argued that Douglas's testimony should have been suppressed on the grounds that the presentation of incentives to Douglas violated Section 201(c)(2) of Title 18 of the US Code prohibiting incentives in exchange for testimony. This part of the code is referred to as the Federal Bribery Statute and states, "Whoever directly or indirectly, corruptly gives, offers, or promises anything of value to any person, with intent to influence the testimony under oath or affirmation, such first mentioned person as a witness upon a trial, hearing, or other proceeding, before any court . . . shall be fined under this title or imprisoned for not more than two years, or both." A three-judge panel of the Tenth Circuit Court of Appeals heard the appeal and on July 1, 1999, ruled that testimony from a witness who had been offered a reduced sentence by a prosecutor in exchange for testimony against a codefendant violated the Federal Bribery Statute and should not be admitted (*Singleton I*). The panel thus ruled that "whoever" could apply to a prosecutor.

The *Singleton I* decision was criticized not on a legal basis but on the grounds that it would make prosecuting cases very difficult (*Frontline*, 1999). Singleton, after all, had been convicted by Douglas's testimony. Thus, on July 10, 1998 (less than two weeks later) the full twelve-member panel of the Tenth Circuit Court decided to rehear this case. In this rehearing (designated *Singleton II*), the panel had a very different interpretation of the Federal Bribery Statute. They ruled that "whoever" could not be deemed to include the sovereign government of the United States and that a "thing of value" cannot be construed to include benefits received from the state (*US v. Singleton*, 1999). Although prosecutors are persons, when they make plea bargains with defendants they act in their official capacity as agents of the US government. Because the US government is not a person, a prosecutor could not be encompassed by the word "whoever." Thus, defining just one word ("whoever") changed the legal definition of the way incentives were handed out and thus opened the door to the continued use of incentives in eliciting and promoting jailhouse informants to work with prosecutors.

The decision in *Singleton II* (*US v. Singleton*, 1999) that allowed incentives has been bolstered over the years by Sentencing Guidelines (Simons, 2003). Specifically, judges are often constrained by mandatory minimum sentencing laws put into place in 1987 (Simons, 2003). The constraints dictate the length of a sentence, with ranges being significantly narrower but typically more severe than pre–Sentencing Guidelines law (Simons, 2003). In addition, the Sentencing Guidelines typically do not allow judges to weight various factors in determining a sentence (e.g., criminal record, life history; Wheeler et al., 1988). Despite these constraints on judges regarding sentencing decisions, Section 5K1.1 of the Sentencing Guidelines allows judges to depart from the guidelines if a defendant has offered substantial assistance in investigating and prosecuting another individual. Of course, jailhouse informants fall within this section. A cooperating witness, such as a jailhouse informant, can receive a lower-than-mandated sentence, and depending on an application filed by the prosecution, the decrease is purely discretionary and cannot be reviewed on appeal (see *US v. Khalil*, 1997).

Allowing judges to offer lower-than-mandated sentences effectively opened the door to providing incentives to jailhouse informants who have an opportunity—likely their only opportunity—to reduce their sentence or gain other benefits through cooperation with the prosecution. Simons (2003) notes that no statistics exist on cooperation of individuals before the guidelines were put into place, but later data offer a glimpse into how the change in the Sentencing Guidelines has increased cooperation. The first year that the Sentencing Commission kept statistics on cooperation was 1989. In this year, 3.5 percent of defendants sentenced under the Sentencing Guidelines received substantial sentence reductions for cooperating (US Sentencing Commission, 1996). Since 1994, the data show that about 20 percent of all federal defendants have received such reductions (US Sentencing Commission, 1996).

Question 5: Does the Fourteenth Amendment prohibit nondisclosure of evidence related to jailhouse testimony?

Although the *Singleton II* ruling (*US v. Singleton*, 1999) and specific sentencing guidelines have allowed prosecutors to offer incentives to jailhouse informants, it is important to note that all evidence, including incentives offered to a jailhouse informant, inculpatory evidence, and impeachment evidence, must be disclosed to the defense if the information is deemed material (i.e., likely to affect a case's outcome) to the guilt or punishment of a defendant. In this way, the disclosure of the evidence guarantees the defendant due process of law (see the Fourteenth Amendment)—the government cannot deprive someone of life, liberty, or property without following certain rules. These rules in criminal trials govern what kind of evidence the government must produce and aim to ensure that every individual receives a fair trial.

We now cover three US Supreme Court rulings (in historical order) regarding the disclosure of evidence to the defense. First, *Brady v. Maryland* (1963) involved a young man, John Brady, found guilty of taking part in a murder and sentenced to death. Brady claimed that his coconspirator (Charles Boblit) did the actual killing. Although the prosecution had a written confession from Boblit, in which he stated that he committed the murder and could have exonerated Brady, the prosecution did not turn over this evidence to the defense. Because of the prosecution's inaction regarding the evidence, Brady appealed his verdict. The Maryland Supreme Court made an interesting ruling in the Brady case: they ruled that by withholding this information from the defense, the prosecutor denied due process to Brady, but only for the punishment portion of his trial. As for the verdict of guilty, they felt turning over Boblit's confession would not have reduced Brady's responsibility below murder in the first degree. The US Supreme Court upheld the Maryland Supreme Court ruling.

The next case involving disclosure of evidence was *Giglio v. US* (1972). This case is more complex. In 1966, Manufacturers Hanover Trust Company discovered that one of their bank tellers, Robert Taliento, had cashed many forged money orders. After being questioned by the FBI, Taliento confessed that he had worked with John Giglio to defraud the bank by cashing the forged money orders. Seeking to reduce his jail term, Taliento struck a deal with Assistant US Attorney DiPaola to testify against Giglio (first at a grand jury hearing) in exchange for immunity from prosecution. Giglio was indicted and went to trial two years later, the case handled by Assistant US Attorney Golden. DiPaola never informed Golden that he had struck a deal with Taliento. In fact, Golden assured Taliento that he would be prosecuted if he did not testify against Giglio. Taliento testified and under oath indicated that he expected to be prosecuted. None of the conversations that Taliento had with DiPaola were disclosed to the defense, and Giglio was convicted for passing forged money orders. While awaiting appeal, Giglio's defense became aware of Taliento's negotiations with the government. The US Supreme Court granted certiorari, a judicial review of a decision of a lower court, to determine if the withholding of the negotiations was a violation of Giglio's due process rights.

The US Supreme Court ruled that regardless of whether DiPaola's failure to disclose the deal with Taliento was intentional or negligent, disclosing exculpatory information is the responsibility of the prosecution. The Court also noted that the prosecution's case relied heavily on Taliento's testimony. Thus, Taliento's credibility was an issue, and the deal that he had with the prosecution was directly relevant to his credibility. As a result, Giglio was granted a new trial, and more importantly, although incentives offered to jailhouse informants were still allowable, they now had to be disclosed to the defense. This ruling stated that it was a due process violation if a prosecutor failed to correct perjured testimony if the prosecutor's office was aware of the lie, even if the individual prosecutor in the courtroom was not aware.

The third case involving disclosing evidence to the defense was *Kyles v. Whitley* (1995; see also *Banks v. Dretke*, 2004). In this murder case, Curtis Lee Kyles was convicted and sentenced to death in Louisiana. After the conviction, it was revealed that the state failed to disclose evidence to the defense, including various statements made to the police by an informant—who did not testify during the trial. Although a state trial court and the State Supreme Court denied Kyles's application for review, Kyles looked for relief at the federal level, claiming his conviction violated *Brady v. Maryland* (1963). After the Federal District Court denied relief and the Fifth Circuit affirmed, the US Supreme Court ruled in favor of Kyles that he should receive a new trial.

In presenting cases describing the importance of the prosecution turning over evidence (including that of informants) to the defense, it is important to also present the case of Cameron Todd Willingham, which serves as an example of the potential consequences when prosecutors do not turn over material evidence. Willingham was convicted of killing his three daughters by setting their home on fire in 1991. He was sentenced to death and executed in 2004. One of the critical pieces of evidence against Willingham was that of a jailhouse informant, Johnny Webb, who testified that Willingham told him that he had committed these killings (Possley, 2015; Schwartz, 2014). On the stand, Webb also testified that he was offered nothing for his testimony. However, evidence collected after Willingham was executed indicated that Webb's parole was handled more quickly than usual, he received clemency for certain crimes, he was moved from state prison back to his hometown jail, and he received money from a local businessman. None of this information was given to Willingham's defense team. In addition, Webb would later recant his testimony that Willingham confessed to setting his house on fire with the toddlers inside (Possley,

2014, 2015; Schwartz, 2014). Because evidence was not presented to the defense, a potentially innocent man was executed.

Although incentive deals made with a jailhouse informant prior to a trial should be disclosed to the defense, it is possible for a jailhouse informant to testify with no assurance of a deal (Simons, 2003). For example, the prosecution may inform a jailhouse informant that a deal may occur only after the jailhouse informant testifies. In this situation, the prosecution may wait to see if the jailhouse informant's testimony is worth "trading" for an incentive. This situation would allow a jailhouse informant to acknowledge in court, technically telling the truth, that they had talked to the prosecution but that no deal was made. This communication between a jailhouse informant and the prosecution would likely not be perceived as unusual, given that all prosecution witnesses talk to the prosecution before a trial.

Summary

This chapter has shown that jailhouse informants are free to testify in court in most trials. This ability is due to rules of evidence developed by judges and passed by Congress (e.g., jailhouse informant testimony is not hearsay) and through interpretations of law made by the US courts, including the US Supreme Court. These legal interpretations have been based on the importance of continuing to protect the rights of a defendant and allow for a fair trial. Of course, this state of fairness in the courtroom is always the ideal, but concerns have been raised that the current legal landscape needs to place more regulations on jailhouse informant testimony (e.g., Merritt, 2003). Without these regulations, the possibility may increase that jailhouse informants may not always be truthful and that jurors may not be able to discriminate true from false testimony. In the next chapter we look at the psychology of both primary and secondary confessions, the latter involving jailhouse informants. We explore the path to confessions, theoretical views on why confessions occur, false confessions, and how confession evidence is perceived in the courtroom.

3

Confession Evidence

Is It Valid?

> In September 2019 Donald Davidson was sentenced to death after a bench trial for the sexual assault and murder of a mother and her ten-year-old child (Rousseau, 2019). Davidson confessed to these murders during a lengthy police interrogation that lasted into the early morning hours. At one point Davidson stated to detectives that he was fatigued and hungry. In addition, during this confession, Davidson's physical and mental condition led him at one point to tell the detectives that he would say whatever they wanted to hear (Schindler, 2019).

A primary confession (i.e., from the defendant himself), like that described above, is a routine result of police work during a criminal investigation. Such a confession is to be distinguished from a secondary confession, in which a jailhouse informant testifies about information confessed to him by a defendant. An example of a secondary confession is the following case:

> On September 19, 1986, Jerry Watkins was convicted of the charges of murder and sexual assault and sentenced to sixty years in prison. His conviction was partly based on the testimony of Dennis Ackeret, a jailhouse informant, who claimed that he had met Watkins in a holding cell and that Watkins confessed to the murder. After serving fourteen years of his sentence, Watkins was released from prison after DNA technology was able to confirm Watkins's innocence. (National Registry of Exonerations, 2017)

In this chapter we focus on the psychology of confessions. We describe research on both primary and secondary confessions that illustrates the similarities and differences between the two. This research includes why confessions occur, theories of confessions, and issues of false confessions through coercion and pressure. In addition, we review the impact of primary confessions in the courtroom in this chapter, and that of secondary confessions in chapter 5.

Both primary and secondary confessions involve a person declaring (orally or in writing) that a crime was committed. The former involves a person acknowledging the crime was committed by *themselves*, whereas the latter has a person (i.e., a jailhouse informant) stating that a crime was committed by *another person* who admitted committing the crime. In addition to this distinction, it is important to note that a primary confession typically leads to an individual harming themselves (i.e., being found guilty), although it is possible that a confession might result in a better outcome than if they went to trial (Bornstein & Neuschatz, 2020). Conversely, a secondary confession results in a positive outcome (e.g., reduced jail time) for the confessor (i.e., a jailhouse informant) and a negative outcome for the person who admitted committing the crime.

Confessions, when true, have tremendous value to the legal system because they lead to guilty pleas and convictions. Still, confessions provoke serious concerns within the legal system related to whether a confession was presented voluntarily and whether it was true (see Kassin, 2015). Regarding the veracity of a confession, one must keep in mind that a confession can be deemed false because (a) it was determined that a crime was not committed; (b) additional evidence showed that the confessor (primary confession) / defendant (secondary confession) could not have committed the crime; (c) another person was arrested and linked to the crime; or (d) additional evidence (e.g., DNA) established the confessor's/defendant's innocence (Kassin et al., 2010).

The Path to a Confession

The path to a primary confession is typically the result of modern police interrogation methods (Inbau et al., 2013; Inbau & Reid, 1962), so named because they are supposed to involve the infliction of physical and/or mental pain to force a suspect to confess (i.e., the third-degree method; see Leo, 2008). Giving someone the "third degree" was deemed a violation of the Fourteenth Amendment by the US Supreme Court in the *Brown v. Mississippi* (1936) decision—any interrogation obtained through force was deemed involuntary and violated the constitutional rights of a defendant.

In the absence of overt abuse, modern interrogators have adopted what Leo has referred to as the psychological third degree (Leo, 2008). These modern methods involve the process of social influence, which is designed to lead suspects to incriminate themselves by increasing the anxiety associated with denial, plunging them into a state of despair, and minimizing the perceived consequences of a confession (Kassin & Gudjonsson, 2004). We should note that although their research is a bit dated, Kassin and Gudjonsson found that the confession rate in the United Kingdom was close to 60 percent, in the United States 42 to 55 percent, and in Japan 90 percent. In addition, one must keep in mind that a suspect may deliberately confess to mitigate their sentence. This possibility was raised as far back as Munsterberg (1908) in the early twentieth century (see Bornstein & Neuschatz, 2020). Munsterberg described a case where two brothers confessed to killing another brother because the evidence against them was overwhelming. Confessing was seen by the brothers as the only way to avoid the death penalty.

There are several paths to a secondary confession, and these are very different from the path to a primary confession described above. Most notable in this regard is that a secondary confession does not involve the direct participation of law enforcement—the confession comes indirectly from a defendant to a jailhouse informant. Thus, there are no pre-interrogation issues, no concern with Miranda rights (*Miranda v.*

Arizona, 1966), and no actual formal interrogation. Any communication between a defendant and a jailhouse informant is strictly one-on-one, with the jailhouse informant claiming to have been told or to have overheard the suspect confess to committing a crime (Neuschatz et al., 2008, Neuschatz et al., 2020).

The transmission of information from a defendant to a jailhouse informant can take many forms. Let us begin with the defendant. First, it is possible that the defendant tells the jailhouse informant accurate information about the case (i.e., truthfully admitting to being involved in a crime). Second, the defendant may tell the jailhouse informant inaccurate information (i.e., boasting). Third, the defendant may talk to the jailhouse informant, but the content of their conversation may never include any information about a criminal case. Fourth, the defendant may talk to the jailhouse informant about the case but categorically deny being involved in any crime. Fifth, the defendant may not talk directly to a jailhouse informant, but the jailhouse informant overhears the defendant. Finally, the defendant may not talk to the jailhouse informant at all.

As for jailhouse informants, it is possible that they will convey accurate information in their testimony. This situation is the goal of all prosecutors, serving in many cases to "seal the deal" on a conviction. However, jailhouse informants may take other paths. They may believe a defendant's confession at face value and be willing to convey this information to the authorities, even if it is false or lacks corroboration. Keep in mind that unlike the police jailhouse informants have relatively few resources (although they do have some, like public records, as noted earlier) to determine if the defendant's confession was accurate. In addition, jailhouse informants may know that the information is false (e.g., the defendant was *not* involved in a crime) but be willing to convey inaccurate information and work hard to convince a public official (e.g., a district attorney) and jury members that a suspect had a legitimate reason for wanting to confess.

Keep in mind that although jailhouse informants will typically testify for the prosecution, there have been instances in which they have testified for the defense. Neuschatz et al.'s (2020) archival study found that nine jailhouse informants were presented by the defense to testify in six of the twenty-eight cases surveyed. Most of these defense jailhouse informants (77.78 percent) provided information concerning the prosecution jailhouse informants. This included testifying about the prosecution jailhouse informants' motive for testifying. Neuschatz et al. found examples of defense jailhouse informants who testified that prosecution jailhouse informants stated they were going to "set up" the defendant to get a significant amount of time cut from their sentences. Other defense jailhouse informants who did not testify about prosecution jailhouse informants did testify about the positive aspects of the defendant's character. Neuschatz et al. found that no defense jailhouse informants stated under oath that they were receiving an incentive for testifying. We should note that when there was a defense jailhouse informant, the prosecution would sometimes attack the credibility of this jailhouse informant.

Regardless of the paths described above, it is important to note that secondary confessions involve indirect participation both of law enforcement and of others in the legal system, working behind the scenes to facilitate the transmission of information from a defendant to a jailhouse informant. Some have argued (see Natapoff, 2009) that law enforcement is intimately involved with all informants, including those in the prison system. As we presented earlier, investigations have uncovered the systematic use of jailhouse informants by public officials. These investigations include the jailhouse informant Leslie Vernon White's infamous *60 Minutes* interview, the Los Angeles County Grand Jury (1990), and the 2011 federal investigation of the prosecutors and the Sheriff's Department in Orange County, California (Queally, 2019).

Theories of Confessions

Over the years, various theories have been proposed for primary confessions. As noted by Kassin and Gudjonsson (2004), these theories share one or more of the following basic ideas that an individual will confess to an interrogator when the individual

1. perceives that the evidence against them is strong
2. needs to relieve feelings of guilt or shame
3. has difficulties coping with the pressures of confinement and interrogation
4. is the target of social-psychological influence
5. primarily focuses on the immediate costs and benefits of their actions rather than on the long-term consequences

We present five theoretical perspectives for primary confessions. First, a psychoanalytic explanation (e.g., Reik, 1959) states that people have an unconscious compulsion to confess in response to a real or imagined transgression. In this manner, a confession serves to overcome feelings of guilt and remorse. Second, some have described confessions as akin to a decision-making process (e.g., Herrnstein, 1997; Irving & Hilgendorf, 1980; see also Ofshe & Leo, 1997) in which a suspect decides (not always correctly) to confess based on their assessment of what will enhance their well-being. Given the stress associated with interrogation, one can understand why a suspect would confess—confessing ends the interrogation. Third, a cognitive-behavioral viewpoint (Gudjonsson, 2003) states that a confession is the result of a suspect's relationship to the environment and those in the environment, as well as the suspect's relationship to the antecedent and consequences of confessing (e.g., expectations about future treatment). Fourth, a social-psychological perspective notes that social influence can have a powerful impact on behavior. For example, an individual may confess because of hearing that others had already confessed (e.g., conformity; see Asch, 1956) or out of obedience to authority (e.g., the police; see Milgram, 1974). Finally, a confession may be the result of self-regulation (e.g., Baumeister & Vohs, 2007) or as Davis and Leo (2012) referred to it "interrogation-related regulation decline" (IRRD). Self-regulation is thought of as a limited resource that involves the controlling of one's thoughts, behaviors, and emotions toward the desired goal. In terms of primary confessions, the goal is to maintain one's innocence. However, during an interrogation, as one gets stressed and fatigued and is denied basic needs, the ability to self-regulate gets depleted. A large body of social-psychological research has demonstrated that taxing physiological, cognitive, and social factors can interfere with the ability to self-regulate (e.g., Baumeister & Vohs, 2007). As one can imagine, a suspect being interrogated might not have the cognitive and emotional resolve to fend off the onslaught of attacks and accusations. As the interrogation continues, the suspect's ability to resist may be depleted and they give up and confess—everyone has their breaking point.

Regarding theoretical explanations for secondary confessions, we must consider both the confession of a defendant to a jailhouse informant and the confession of a jailhouse informant to the authorities. We believe that for a defendant, of the five factors that likely lead to a primary confession, two do *not* apply to a secondary confession: a defendant who tells a jailhouse informant about a crime they committed is unlikely to be concerned about strong evidence collected by the prosecution, nor is this defendant focused on the immediate costs and benefits of their actions rather than long-term consequences. However, the defendant may need to relieve feelings of guilt or shame about committing a crime (i.e., "get it off my chest"). In addition, the stress and fatigue of confinement and isolation for a defendant may be exhausting and jeopardize their ability to self-regulate (Baumeister & Vohs, 2007; Davis & Leo, 2012) and maintain the goal of not talking while incarcerated. To the extent that another inmate is continually asking them about their crime, maybe with the promise of helping, the exhausted defendant may confess to their fellow inmate (i.e., "I had to tell someone"). Finally, the suspect may also feel that telling a jailhouse informant serves a long-term goal of being accepted by peers, especially if the jailhouse informant shares a similar disclosure or if the jailhouse informant is high within the prisoner hierarchy.

As far as what motivates a jailhouse informant to provide a secondary confession to authorities, two possibilities have been raised, both of which have been the focus of research concerning legal decision making in cases involving jailhouse informant testimony. First, a jailhouse informant may provide a secondary confession because of dispositional (internally motivated) factors (Neuschatz et al., 2020). Dispositional factors typically involve aspects of one's personality, such as honesty or compassion. For example, the jailhouse informant may feel badly for the victim(s) of a crime and thus feel it is important to have the perpetrator of the crime locked away.

Second, there are situational factors, the key to which involves incentives. As stated earlier, many jailhouse informants are not providing information to the authorities out of the goodness of their hearts. Instead, they are willing to approach and be approached by the authorities because they will receive some reward (i.e., positive reinforcement) for their testimony. In this way, the situation is the main factor in causing the jailhouse informant to testify. Keep in mind that reward can involve making life in prison more bearable (e.g., additional/better food, increased visitation, or recreational privileges), having one's prison sentence reduced, getting out of prison through parole, or having charges dropped. As noted by Natapoff (2009), the justice system is not averse to rewarding informants for what is deemed "critical" information, even if the rewards handed out cannot ensure that the jailhouse informant is providing accurate information. As we have seen, these rewards may entice a jailhouse informant to come forward with false information. In general, there is no clear punishment for jailhouse informants if they lie; Natapoff (2009) notes that it is rare for a jailhouse informant to be charged with perjury.

The ease of motivating an individual to provide a secondary confession because of an incentive has been shown in the lab by Swanner et al. (2010) using a computer crash paradigm (see Kassin & Kiechel, 1996). Participants were assigned to be a reader or a typist. Some of the readers were provided with false evidence that the typist had confessed to hitting a particular key that caused the computer to crash. Other participants were provided with an incentive (extra experimental credit) to provide evidence against the typist. The results showed that 79 percent of the readers were willing to sign a statement that the typist had admitted to the reader that they hit the key that caused the computer to crash (i.e., secondary confession) versus 52 percent of the typists signing a confession that they themselves had caused the computer crash (i.e., primary confession). These values increased when readers received an incentive. A second experiment by Swanner et al. had a confederate serve as the typist and either confess to or deny hitting the forbidden key. In this experiment, the rate of secondary confessions increased only in the presence of a denial. Swanner et al. showed not only that incentive is critical to secondary confessions but also that these confessions will occur regardless of whether they are true or false.

In another laboratory study investigating secondary confessions and incentives, Jenkins et al. (2021) presented participants with role-playing vignettes that informed them they were being charged with tax evasion. In addition, they were told that they were going to be placed in a cell next to an inmate charged with murder. The participants were not told they should talk to the inmate about the murder charge but were told that they would simply be asked if the inmate had talked to them at all. In this role-playing context, participants were offered various opportunities to make a deal with a prosecutor and work with the government by falsely implicating another inmate. Four offers were manipulated, ranging from a sentence reduction of one year to full immunity. Across three experiments, students (Experiment 1) and community members (Experiments 2 and 3) were willing to assume the role of a jailhouse informant in approximately 25 percent of the cases and provide false evidence against an inmate in exchange for an incentive (see also Robertson & Winkelman, 2017).

False Confessions

Although the interrogation techniques described above elicit primary confessions at a relatively high level, they may not always lead to true primary confessions (see Kassin, Drizin, et al., 2010). In fact, there is considerable evidence showing that interrogation techniques can lead to false primary confessions (see Garrett, 2011; Munsterberg, 1908). Some false primary confessions are voluntary, the result of an individual looking for notoriety or perhaps lacking the ability to distinguish fact and fantasy (see Kassin & Gudjonsson, 2004). For example, in 2006 John Mark Karr confessed to killing six-year-old JonBenét Ramsey in 1996, although his DNA was not found on the victim's clothes—the case remains unsolved (Millstein, 2016). As noted by Kassin (2015), other false primary confessions may be the result of high-pressure interrogation techniques (e.g., continual interruptions, cutting off denials). Finally, some false primary confessions are due to internalization (an individual comes to believe they committed an act; see Kassin, 2007). An example of internalization is the case of Billy Wayne Cope, who falsely confessed to raping and killing his daughter; the case is described in detail by Kassin (2007).

Regardless of the reason, false primary confessions may lead to false convictions—a major problem for our legal system. There are many examples of the impact of false primary confessions in the legal system (see Drizin & Leo, 2004, Garrett, 2011). Here is one, the case of the Central Park Five (BBC News, 2019; Cook, 2019).

> Trisha Meili, a twenty-nine-year-old white woman, went jogging on the night of April 19, 1989, in Central Park. She was found several hours later, close to death (having been brutally beaten and raped) in a ravine. Her attack was one of several to occur in Central Park that night as a group of thirty teenagers (thirteen to seventeen years old) were suspected of assaulting other citizens. The police viewed Meili's attack as part of the assaults committed that night, and they arrested several teenagers in con-

nection with the crimes. Ultimately, five of the boys (African American and Hispanic) were interrogated for many hours; none had counsel present. Four of the five confessed to the attack on Meili and were charged in this rape and assault case. As noted by Nesterak (2014), none of the five confessed to raping the jogger, and each implicated the others, stating he himself was only minimally involved in the attack. It was later revealed that the interrogations involved tactics (e.g., physical force, aggressive questioning, shouting, threats, and lies) to get them to confess. For example, one defendant, Yusef Salaam, stated that "police deprived us of food, drink or sleep for more than 24 hours" (Salaam, 2016). In addition, the boys thought they could go home if they told the police what they wanted to hear. It should be noted that the confessions were videotaped, but there were no recordings of questioning prior to the confessions (CBS News, 2019). The five soon recanted their confessions. Although there was no physical evidence (including DNA) linking them to the crime, the five were prosecuted by the New York City District Attorney and convicted. In 2002, after serving part of their prison sentence, they were all released when a murderer and serial rapist confessed to the attack and his DNA matched with that found on the jogger (Story, 2019).

Secondary confessions may also lead to false testimony in court. How often this occurs is unclear, given that no data exist (that we know of) that indicate the number of truthful versus untruthful jailhouse informants who have testified. Despite the absence of data, it seems likely that some jailhouse informants have been truthful on the stand. Regarding untruthful jailhouse informants, we know (and will present data below) that some jailhouse informant testimony was false based on additional evidence that exonerated a defendant. We should note, however, that determining the truthfulness of a jailhouse informant may be a function of how a jailhouse informant obtained information from a defendant. For example, if the information was obtained in a coercive manner (e.g., threats, physical violence), one might question the truthfulness of a jailhouse informant's testimony.

Thus far in our book we have presented several examples to illustrate when jailhouse informants have presented false testimony and exonerations resulted. To this point, the Northwestern University School of Law's Center on Wrongful Convictions reviewed the cases of 111 persons released from death row between 1973 and 2004 after being exonerated (Warden, 2004). The center found false testimony from jailhouse informants in more than about 46 percent of those cases. The Innocence Project has also documented that jailhouse informant testimony has contributed to more than 17 percent of wrongful convictions later overturned through DNA testing (Innocence Project, 2019). In these cases, a statement from an informant with an incentive to testify tended to be the evidence that sealed the conviction. Additional psychology and law research support these investigations. Neuschatz et al. (2020) examined archival data and content-analyzed trial records from twenty-two DNA exoneration cases involving fifty-three informants and twenty-eight defendants convicted of serious felonies. They found that most of the jailhouse informants (a) had previously testified for the prosecution and had extensive criminal histories (75 percent) and (b) were not questioned about their history of testifying in other trials (68.95 percent).

Concerns about jailhouse informants providing false testimony raise two critical questions about these secondary confessions. First, what is the nature of the interactions between a defendant and a jailhouse informant? Neuschatz et al. (2020) found that jailhouse informants in exonerated cases (a) had the opportunity to converse with or hear the defendant because they were in the same cell or prison area and had some type of relationship with the defendant and (b) most commonly (43.75 percent) claimed that the defendants confessed after being directly asked whether they were guilty, although others stated that the defendant confessed on their own without any questions (25 percent) or that they overheard the defendant confess to someone else (19 percent). It is unknown whether jailhouse informants were telling the truth about their interactions with defendants.

Second, what is the content of a secondary confession? As stated earlier, a secondary confession involves secondhand information. That is, unlike a primary confession, a jailhouse informant is retelling what was said by someone else. Ideally, a defendant tells a jailhouse informant accurate information and the informant's memory for that information is also accurate. However, it may be that a defendant tells a jailhouse informant a minimum amount of information and the informant embellishes what they were told when testifying in court. This embellishment can take the form of adding false information or adding true details gleaned from public sources (e.g., TV, newspaper, Internet—see the case of Leslie Vernon White). Neuschatz et al. (2020) examined the content of the testimony of thirty-two jailhouse informants in exonerated cases and found that the jailhouse informant testimony included many details about the crime in question. About 65 percent of the details were accurate, but 12.81 percent were inaccurate. Moreover, 85 percent of the jailhouse informants denied having heard any of these details from sources (e.g., TV, newspaper) other than the defendant. However, only 14.29 percent of the jailhouse informants testified to accurate details that the public would never have seen.

It is also important to note that jailhouse informants may present inconsistent testimony. Neuschatz et al. (2020) found that jailhouse informants did so in 64.29 percent of the cases reviewed. The inconsistency was between the jailhouse informant's current testimony and the actual case facts, between the jailhouse informant's current and previous testimony, or between the jailhouse informant's current testimony and what they had previously reported to the police or prosecutor. For example, in the trial of Dennis Williams and Willie Rainge, a jailhouse informant continually mixed up what he allegedly heard each defendant confess. The jailhouse informant's original police report and his direct examination noted that he heard Williams state that he had hidden a weapon. However, during cross-examination, the jailhouse informant switched the details and stated that he heard Rainge claim to have hidden the weapon. The jailhouse informant switched back who had the weapon one more time during his testimony (*People v. Rainge*, 1978). How the inclusion of accurate details by a jailhouse informant amid inconsistency in testimony impacts jurors will be discussed in the next chapter.

Research has shown why false confession testimony can be problematic in the courtroom—it is very believable. Appleby et al. (2013, Experiment 1) analyzed twenty false primary confessions (deemed false by DNA, a dismissal of all charges, an acquittal, or an overturned conviction) that were presented as evidence in court. This analysis showed the difficulty confronted by jurors when faced with a false primary confession—most false confessions seem very real. The study found that false primary confessions often included (a) assertions that the accused confession was voluntary; (b) rich details, including the "what, how, and why" of the crime; (c) the confessor speaking introspectively, reflecting on their own thoughts and feelings at the time of the crime; (d) a theme of minimization that psychologically justified the crime in question; and (e) the confessor expressing sorrow and/or remorse about having committed the crime. The content of false primary confession contributes to the general difficulty individuals have of detecting deception (see Vrij, 2008; Vrij et al., 2011) and to the possibility that other evidence might be interpreted incorrectly based on the false confession (e.g., perceptions of eyewitnesses; see Kassin, 2015).

Beyond the inability to detect deception very well, as noted earlier, jurors also often fall prey to the fundamental attribution error (Gilbert & Malone, 1995; Jones, 1990), tending to make dispositional attributions (attributing a confession to the confessor's own disposition or actions rather than to the confessor's circumstances or situation). These dispositional attributions are quick and relatively automatic and result in jurors *not* acknowledging the possibility that situational forces impacted the truthfulness of the confession (Gilbert & Malone, 1995).

Perceptions of Primary Confessions

As far as courtroom confessions, in the past there were no guidelines regulating the admission of such evidence at trial (see Wigmore, 1970), but now confessions are accepted by a presiding judge on a case-by-case basis. Also, the admission of confession evidence today requires an evaluation based on the "totality of circumstances," and each confession is required to be voluntary (e.g., not elicited by sleep deprivation; *Doody v. Shriro*, 2010). It should also be noted that a judge does not have to present any special instructions to a jury about confession evidence, but a judge can instruct a jury to make an independent judgment of voluntariness and disregard any statements the jury thinks were coerced (see Kamisar et al., 2003).

What does the public think about primary confession evidence? In general, survey research into this question (Chojnacki et al., 2007; Costanzo et al., 2010; Henkel et al., 2008; Kassin et al., 2005; Redlich et al., 2009) has shown that the public has a limited understanding of issues related to primary confessions, including limited understanding of risk factors and interrogation practices that contribute to false confessions (Henkel et al., 2008), and that situational pressure of interrogation would result in false confessions (Costanzo et al., 2010; Henkel et al., 2008).

Regarding the impact of primary confessions in the courtroom, laboratory research has shown not only the influence that primary confessions can have in the context of legal decision making but also the underlying mechanisms that lead individuals to rely on primary confession evidence when rendering a verdict. Before discussing specific primary confession research, it is important to describe the main research methodology for investigating the impact of both primary and secondary confessions on legal decision making. In the laboratory, most studies investigating confessions and legal decision making have used a mock trial methodology. Researchers generate plausible case scenarios, most often based on real-life cases. The scenarios are presented in various contexts—vignette, trial summary, trial transcript, audio trial, or video trial. The scenarios include various components (e.g., legally appropriate charges, realistic witnesses and admissible evidence, and jury instructions) that allow for a high degree of ecological validity (i.e., realism). It should be noted, however, that a laboratory study is still an artificial context—one's ability to generalize from a mock trial to an actual case is decreased (Diamond, 1997; Weiten & Diamond, 1979). The verdict rendered by mock jurors has no impact on a defendant, and serving as a mock juror is not the same as serving as an actual juror (see also Bornstein et al., 2017; Bornstein & McCabe, 2005).

However, despite its artificiality, laboratory research offers critical experimental control that ensures scientific integrity. Researchers design studies that manipulate (vary) specific factors (e.g., the presence of confession evidence) and control (keep constant) all other variables (type of crime) to allow them to draw definitive conclusions about the effects of the manipulated factors. The ability to control all other variables is impossible in an actual courtroom, given that each case varies in unique and numerous ways. Thus, it is important for laboratory research to provide the best available evidence on important legal questions whenever possible (see Goodman et al., 1992).

A few points should be noted about the specifics of laboratory research that uses a mock trial methodology. First, this research typically involves mock *juror* studies and not mock *jury* studies. The former involves collecting data from individual participants role-playing as individual jurors, whereas the latter involves collecting data from a group of participants role-playing as an entire jury. Ideally, a researcher would prefer to conduct a mock jury study since juries rather than individual jurors render (after careful group deliberations) the verdicts of court cases in the real world (see Miller et al., 2011; Moscovici & Zavalloni, 1969; Myers & Bishop, 1970; Nunez et al., 2011; Shaw & Skolnick, 1995). However, an examination of psychology and law journals finds that most published mock trial studies are mock juror studies. This is generally because of (a) cost (i.e., fewer participants are required); (b) efficiency (i.e., not having to recruit a group of people at the same time at a specific location); and

(c) research that suggests that pre-deliberation individual verdicts often match jury verdicts and has also shown that deliberations simply reveal the positions of most jurors rather than changing them (Haegerich & Bottoms, 2004; Kalven & Zeisel, 1966; Sandys & Dillehay, 1995).

Second, participants in mock juror studies have varied. Undergraduates (receiving course credit) were the participants of choice in the past, although there was some research that used paid community members. More recently, mock trial research has recruited community members by using online services such as Mechanical Turk (owned by Amazon.com) and Qualtrics.com. We should note that there has been prolonged debate about using students versus community members—students are viewed as less representative of the population and less scientifically valid (Weiten & Diamond, 1979; Wiener et al., 2011). However, recent meta-analyses (Bornstein et al., 2017; Devine & Caughlin, 2014) have shown consistency in participant samples and consistency in samples run as part of different experiments in the same overall study (e.g., Golding et al., 2016).

Third, in laboratory research participants (typically as part of a between-participants design) are presented a single case in written form as a short vignette, trial summary, or trial transcript (Kassin & Neumann, 1997; Schuller & Stewart, 2000). More recently, this presentation has taken place via programs such as Qualtrics.com or Surveymonkey.com (e.g., Golding et al., 2016; Lynch et al., 2013). Some studies have used audio or video mock trials or parts of mock trials (Spanos et al., 1989), but these have become rare in recent years, likely due to the points raised above about mock juror versus mock jury research. Moreover, a recent meta-analysis found that mock trial studies using different media showed minimal differences between video trials and trials presented as text (Bornstein et al., 2017).

Finally, participants in mock trial research typically make explicit judgments about a case. These include rendering a verdict and/or making other outcome judgments such as credibility ratings (Wenger & Bornstein, 2006). In addition, some studies include open-ended questions assessing reason(s) for a verdict or perceptions of other aspects of the trial (e.g., Lippert et al., 2017).

Having presented the above background on legal decision-making research, we now turn to legal decision-making research involving primary confessions. The initial investigation in this area was done by Kassin and Wrightsman (1980). The study tested the US Supreme Court's assumption that jurors will discount a coerced confession as unreliable and will not allow it to influence their decisions. In this two-experiment study, participants read a trial transcript in which a defendant had confessed (a) of his own accord (no constraint), (b) due to an offer of leniency (positive constraint), or (c) due to a threat of punishment (negative constraint). There was also a control group in which there was no confession. The results showed that participants discounted confessions that involved a negative constraint but that they increased their estimates of the likelihood that the defendant committed the crime when the confession involved either no constraint or a positive constraint. Later studies showed that mock jurors were willing to believe a confession that was the result of a promise of leniency, even though they were specifically admonished to discount an involuntary confession (Kassin & Wrightsman, 1981). The continued use of an involuntary confession was also shown in a mock jury study (six-person juries) that included deliberations (Kassin & Wrightsman, 1985).

This early study on the impact of primary confessions in the courtroom was followed by many others. For example, Kassin and Neumann (1997) compared the impact of confession evidence to other types of evidence. In this way, Kassin and Neumann could evaluate the US Supreme Court's claim in *Arizona v. Fulminante* (1991) that confessions were not fundamentally different from other types of evidence. In three experiments, the results showed that confession evidence led to the highest conviction rates across various types of trials (e.g., murder, rape, assault, and theft in Experiment 1) compared to other types of evidence—eyewitness identification, character testimony, or no other evidence. Additional research showed that individuals may be influenced by confession evidence regardless of whether they judged the confession to be voluntary or coerced. For example, in Kassin and Sukel (1997) participants were presented with one of three versions of a murder trial. In a low-pressure confession condition, the defendant confessed to police immediately upon questioning, and in a high-pressure confession condition, the defendant was in pain and interrogated aggressively by a detective who waved his gun menacingly. For both conditions, there were instructions from a judge that either admitted the confession testimony or ruled it inadmissible. The third condition in this experiment was a control version in which there was no confession evidence. Kassin and Sukel found that jurors rated the high-pressure condition as leading to a less voluntary confession and rated it as having less influence on their decisions than the low-pressure condition. Despite this, when participants' verdicts were recorded, any confession, whether perceived as voluntary or coerced, increased the conviction rate compared to the control condition. Moreover, this increase occurred even when the confession was ruled inadmissible. Similar findings have been reported by Wallace and Kassin (2012) in a study using actual judges as participants.

As for why actual and mock jurors are more likely to be influenced by primary confession evidence than other types of evidence, Kassin (2015) offered two reasons, both of which will be critical to the discussion of research on perceptions of secondary confessions in chapter 5. First, most people believe that they would never confess to a crime they did not commit, evaluate others accordingly, and have only rudimentary understanding of the dispositional and situational factors that would lead someone to confess (Henkel et al., 2008; Leo & Liu, 2009). Second, people believe that only someone who confessed to a crime would know details about a case (Leo & Drizen, 2010).

Summary

This chapter has illustrated the unique issues that arise when the legal system must deal with confessions. These issues include how confessions are obtained (whether primary or secondary) and theoretical views of what might underlie an individual confessing to the police (primary confession) or a fellow inmate (secondary confession). In addition, we have examined the possibility that a confession may be false, either because of pressure during an interrogation or because a jailhouse informant was not actually told information by another inmate. Finally, we presented research that illustrated how confessions are perceived, making clear that confession evidence has a large impact on jurors deciding a case.

In the next chapter, we examine lying and abilities to detect deception.

4

Detecting Deception

As we have seen, jailhouse informants have been shown to present false testimony in court. However, their testimony is often believed by jurors because they are often unable to detect deception. Take the case of Curtis Flowers.

In Winona, Mississippi, in the early morning of July 16, 1996, an unknown gunman walked into the Tardy Furniture store and shot and killed four people: the owner, Bertha Tardy, and three of her employees. A young African American man, Curtis Flowers, became the center of the investigation. Prosecutors argued that Flowers killed Tardy and her employees because he was angry that he was fired and that his pay was docked in order to repay for merchandise he had damaged. Flowers would eventually be convicted of the murders. In fact, Flowers had six trials, which included three different jailhouse informants: Fredrick Veal, Maurice Hawkins, and Odell Hallmon. Eventually, all three jailhouse informants admitted their stories were fictitious (Yesko, 2019). Flowers was tried six times because each one of his convictions was overturned for different reasons, such as prosecutorial misconduct; the fourth and fifth trials ended with hung juries. In the sixth trial he was convicted of four counts of capital murder and sentenced to death. In September 2020, the convictions were overturned, and the Mississippi Attorney General's Office dismissed all charges. In all, Curtis Flowers endured twenty-three years in prison, six trials, and four death penalties.

Frederick Veal, one of the jailhouse informants in the Curtis Flowers case, told law enforcement that Flowers confessed to him during a late-night conversation, while jailhouse informant Maurice Hawkins stated that Flowers's confession occurred over a card game. Both jailhouse informants testified at only the first trial, providing important evidence that would help convict Flowers (Yesko, 2019). Flowers was convicted of murder and given the death sentence. Both Veal and Hawkins later admitted in a signed affidavit that Flowers had never confessed to them. In an interview with *APM Reports* (Yesko, 2019), Veal specifically stated that he was looking to get a deal from the district attorney in the form of reward money and was willing to make up a story about Flowers to get it. In fact, as reported by *APM Reports* (Yesko, 2019), Veal indicated that the authorities intentionally housed him with Flowers so he could get a confession from Flowers. Veal added that he was promised a share of a thirty-thousand-dollar reward for Flowers's conviction if he testified and that he had already made plans as to how he and Hawkins would spend the money by the time the first trial took place. By their own admission, both Hawkins and Veal perjured themselves but were ultimately believed by the jury.

The final jailhouse informant, Hallmon, fit the prototype. He was a career criminal facing a lengthy jail term and according to *APM Reports* (Yesko, 2019) was a confidential informant for the police. Hallmon testified at Flowers's third trial (and trials 4–6) that Flowers confessed to him in jail, and this testimony was the only direct evidence that linked Flowers to the crime. It should be noted that in Flowers's second trial Hallmon testified as a defense witness. He claimed that an inculpatory letter about Flowers written by Hallmon's sister contained falsehood and that she was motivated to write it only for the reward money. However, by the third trial Hallmon had been arrested on drug charges and gave testimony for the prosecution and testified that he had perjured himself in the second trial. He also testified that Flowers had confessed to him in jail. Given the switching of sides, Flowers's attorney (Ray Charles) petitioned the court to exclude Hallmon's testimony on the basis that it was unreliable. After all, Hallmon had admitted that he perjured himself in the second trial. Despite the defense petition, the judge in the third trial ruled in favor of the prosecution and allowed Hallmon to testify. According to *APM Reports* (Yesko, 2019), while Flowers was waiting in jail after the third trial, Hallmon was released from prison and continued to commit serious crimes such as selling drugs, attempting to run over a sheriff's deputy, and committing assault. Despite these criminal acts, Hallmon continued to receive deals from the district attorney for serving as a jailhouse informant. These deals allowed Hallmon to serve relatively little time in jail. Hallmon himself told *APM Reports* (Yesko, 2019) that even he was surprised that he was not charged when he attempted to run over the sheriff's deputy. Hallmon's crimes continued until he eventually committed a spree of three murders that included his girlfriend, whom he murdered in front of their child. He also attempted to kill his son but was unsuccessful.

The Flowers case and especially the conduct of jailhouse informant Hallmon exemplify the problems of offering incentives to jailhouse informants to testify; their testimony might be false. Hallmon was a self-admitted liar, even after taking an oath to testify truthfully in the third trial. For example, he explained on the witness stand that he lied in the second trial at the behest of Flowers, saying he agreed to testify on Flowers's behalf in exchange for cigarettes and money. When Hallmon was contacted for an interview by *APM Reports*, he admitted that Flowers never confessed to him, and his testimony was indeed false in trials 3–6. In Hallmon's words, "It was a complete fantasy" (Yesko, 2019). In addition, Hallmon stated that he had struck a deal with the district attorney, receiving relief for his crimes in exchange for his testimony against Flowers. Hallmon indicated that his drug charges were dismissed because the district attorney stated that he would rather have a murderer (Flowers) than a drug dealer (Hallmon) in jail. This contradicts Hallmon's trial testimony, in which he testified under oath that he was never awarded a deal in exchange for his testimony and claimed that the only reason he testified was because his conscience bothered him. When contacted by *APM Reports* for an interview, Hallmon asked to be paid for his interview (Yesko, 2019).

The Flowers case raises a critical question: why did the jury believe the jailhouse informants, especially Hallmon? One answer is that individuals find it difficult to detect deception (Vrij, 2008). This difficulty is increased when the deceptive party, like Hallmon and other jailhouse informants, are experienced liars and mix truths with their lies (Vrij et al., 2010). Jailhouse informants are often practiced and comfortable liars whose testimony generally fits the fact pattern of a crime—hardly any prosecutor would put on the stand a witness whose testimony was grossly inaccurate. The aspect of jailhouse informant testimony that is most likely false is *how* they obtained information about the crime; this was the case with the initial jailhouse informants in the Flowers trial (Veal and Hawkins).

In the section that follows, we discuss the difficulties in detecting deception. We start with the concepts of the lie base rate and truth bias. The lie base rate is the average number of lies the typical person tells over time such as a day or week. Truth bias is the name for the phenomenon in which people are likely to believe that others are truthful unless they are given a reason to suspect they are being deceived (Levine et al., 1999). We show that beyond a few prolific liars, most people do not regularly lie. We follow with a discussion of the stereotypes and beliefs people have about verbal and nonverbal cues to deception and how these mistaken beliefs lead to inaccurate decisions about the truthfulness of a person. Finally, we conclude by indicating how the lie base rate, the truth bias, and the perceived cues to deception conspire to make it more difficult for jurors to effectively determine when jailhouse informants are lying on the witness stand.

Lie Base Rates and Truth Bias

It is important to define a few terms before reviewing the truth bias literature and how it relates to jailhouse informants. First, note that there is technically a difference between deception and lying. Levine (2014) defines deception as intentionally misleading others, whereas lying is a type of deception that involves a falsehood known by the teller. For this chapter, the terms will be used interchangeably. A truth, on the other hand, occurs in any communication where there is no intent to deceive or mislead. Levine argues that people have a truth bias because most of our interactions are truthful; we do not spend much time scrutinizing others' statements. This assumption is problematic when people are lying or, sometimes in the case of jailhouse informants, giving false testimony.

The notion that individuals do not often lie is consistent with Grice's (1991) logic of conversation—that most people presume that communication is cooperative. There have been several studies designed to measure the number of times people lie, otherwise known as the lie base rate (see Serota et al., 2010). For the most part these studies have arrived at similar conclusions—people do not lie often. Therefore, it makes sense that most people, in the words of Grice (1991), trust that communication is cooperative and not deceptive.

One of the first studies to investigate the frequency of lying was conducted by DePaulo et al. (1996), in which participants were instructed to record each time they lied in a diary. DePaulo et al. were interested in the number of lies per day reported by both students (Experiment 1) and community members (Experiment 2). Participants were instructed to record any lies they told in interactions with others that lasted ten minutes or longer; lies were operationally defined as any attempt to mislead. DePaulo et al. reported the mean number of lies per day was 1.96 for the students and 0.97 for the nonstudents. When the data were broken down by gender, there were no significant differences in the number of lies; men and women lied equally often in their social interactions. Participants reported that they lied less frequently than they expected they would and that they believed they lied less often than others their age. No matter the beliefs about the frequency of lying, participants did not report lying much at all, fewer than two times per day in social interactions lasting more than ten minutes.

Based on the above study's results, it could be conjectured that people lie more often in short social interactions (less than ten minutes) because they may want to exit the situation after being untruthful or because shorter interactions allow for more opportunities to lie since there are more of them in a day. George and Robb (2008) also conducted a diary study where they varied the amount of time that constituted a social interaction from ten minutes (Experiment 1) to five minutes (Experiment 2). Participants reported more lies per day in a five-minute social interaction (M = 0.90) than in a ten-minute social interaction (M = 0.59). Even though people lied more when the social interaction was shorter, these results largely confirm the findings of DePaulo et al. (1996). The two studies together suggest the base rate of lying ranges from approximately 0.60 to 1.96 lies per day.

The two studies just described (DePaulo et al., 1996; George & Robb, 2008) both had small samples, calling into question the generalizability of the results. DePaulo et al. (1996) had only 147 participants total (n = 77 in Experiment 1 and n = 70 in Experiment 2), and George and Robb (2008) had 24 participants. However, a national cross-sectional survey involving 1,000 respondents also supported the low frequency of daily lying (Serota et al., 2010). In this survey, participants were asked how many times they had lied in the previous twenty-four hours. Those who lied were asked a follow-up question about whom they lied to, whether it was family members, business associates, friends, acquaintances, or strangers. In addition, they were asked for each type of acquaintance, whether the deception was done in person or through some electronic medium (it might be easier to lie when you are not face-to-face with the person you are trying to deceive). The average number of lies reported per day was 1.65, which replicated what had been found in prior research (Serota et al., 2010). Whether the lie was face-to-face or through an electronic medium had no effect on the frequency of lying.

The Serota et al. (2010) results were qualified when the authors examined the distribution of lies per participant instead the averaged data. This analysis revealed that most of the sample (approximately 60 percent) reported no lies at all over the twenty-four-hour period. Of the 400 lies that were reported, 22 percent were told by 1 percent of the sample and half of the lies were told by a little over 5 percent of the sample. The authors concluded that most people do not lie daily and that there are only a few prolific liars who lie considerably more than the average person. It may be that some jailhouse informants are prolific liars: certainly, the prolific jailhouse informants White, Fink, and Hallmon lied over and over.

To ascertain if the survey results were consistent with DePaulo et al. (1996) and George and Robb (2008), Serota et al. (2010) reanalyzed both earlier data sets to test if the lies were predominantly told by a few participants in these studies as well. These reanalyses replicated Serota et al.'s national survey. For example, in the George and Robb data set, twenty-three of the twenty-four participants reported lying over a weeklong period, and the average number of lies was 0.90, or less than one per day. Three out of the twenty-four total participants told over a quarter of the lies reported. Once again, the base rate for lying is very low, except for a few prodigious liars. These results have also been replicated in a sample of US high school students (Levine et al., 2013) and in a large, representative UK community sample (Serota et al., 2012).

It is possible that more people lie daily than was reported in the Serota studies (Serota et al., 2010; Serota et al., 2012), but they did not report it accurately. There are a variety of reasons why this could be true: the participants could have innocently forgotten to report (anyone who keeps a food diary on their phone can relate to forgetting to record what they ate), or they could have been unwilling to report lying because it would present them in an undesirable light. Serota et al. (2010) were concerned about these possibilities and attempted to address them by replicating the survey results in the laboratory. Participants were given the same survey that was given to the participants in the national studies, with an exception: rather than being forced to respond to every question in the survey, as was required in the national survey, participants could skip questions that were not applicable, and if they indicated that they had not lied in the time specified in the question, they were asked to report the last time they lied. The results were very similar to the national sample (Serota et al., 2010), although the college sample (Serota et al., 2010) lied a bit more than the national sample ($M = 2.34$ lies per day).

Once again, most lies were told by a few participants. Thus, these results demonstrated that participants were likely not lying or failing to report on the other studies.

In a more rigorous test of the self-report data of Serota et al. (2010), Halevy et al. (2014) correlated self-reported lying with other measures of deceptive behavior. Halevy et al. first replicated the general findings of Serota et al. (2010) with a survey sample of five hundred Dutch college students. Then they selected a subset of this sample, those who self-reported lying, to complete the experimental task. This task incentivized them to lie for financial gain. In one task, participants were given a die inside a paper cup. The cup had a small hole that allowed the participant to roll the die under the cup and privately see the outcome. Participants were told that higher numbers, such as 5 or 6, would result in greater monetary reward. Participants were instructed to report the roll. Lying was analyzed by comparing the combined data from all participants to the theoretic distribution of an honest die roll. As expected, lying was correlated with cheating, meaning that people who lied were also likely to cheat. The authors interpreted the results to be a conceptual replication of Serota et al.—most people are honest and do not lie much at all.

The result that most people do not lie has been consistently found in the laboratory and on surveys, across varied samples and procedures (Halevy et al., 2014; Levine et al., 2011; Serota et al., 2012). That is, the base rate of lying is very low except for a few people who are habitual liars. Given that the lying base rate is so low, it makes sense that most will assume, as a default, that others are truthful in their communication (Levine, 2014). If people do not lie often, then the assumption that a speaker is truthful will be correct most of the time. Levine's (2014) truth-default theory (TDT) states that people are in a "truth default state" unless they have a reason to believe they are being deceived; they have what is called a "truth bias." A truth bias is just what the name implies—a tendency to judge a message as truthful regardless of its actual veracity (Levine, 2014).

The phenomenon of the truth bias has been confirmed empirically by Bond and DePaulo (2006) in what is to date the most extensive meta-analysis on detecting deception. Overall, they analyzed 206 studies that included 24,483 participants.[1] These studies contained participants who had no special training in discriminating truth from lies. Bond and DePaulo found that participants were able to correctly classify truth and lies 54 percent of the time—a little over half the time. Participants accurately classified lies 47 percent of the time and thought lies were true 54 percent of the time. In contrast, truths were accurately classified as nondeceptive 61 percent of the time. Thus, there is a bias to judge statements as truthful.

In deception detection experiments, such as those included in the meta-analysis by Bond and DePaulo (2006) described above, participants (by design) were specifically asked to make truth-lie judgments. As evident in the meta-analysis, the truth bias was pervasive. In some studies, such as McCornack and Levine (1990), researchers examined the truth bias when the true nature of the experiment was hidden from the participant and the participant was unlikely to suspect deception—or in what the authors referred to as a "low state of suspicion for detection." In a low state suspicion condition, subjects rated the veracity of a videotape interview of their romantic partner but were not given any information about deception. In the other condition, participants were explicitly told to expect deception. McCornack and Levine found that the truth bias was even higher in the low state suspicion condition for truth-lie judgments (M = 80 percent) as opposed to more explicit conditions (64 percent). This suggests that the truth bias may be underestimated in the laboratory and more pervasive in everyday conversation because in everyday life people do not expect deception and are therefore less likely to detect it.

Even when a message is implausible or when people have a reason to be suspicious of the message, people still unremittingly exhibit a truth bias, although it is not as pronounced. For example, Clare and Levine (2019) tested whether the truth bias would still occur under conditions of implicit prompting and implausible deceptions. To this end, participants watched videotaped interviews of a typical self-disclosure task in which the confederate being interviewed responded with an equal amount of truthful and untruthful answers. In addition, participants were exposed to plausible and implausible truths and lies. An example of an implausible lie offered by Clare and Levine might be that brussels sprouts is a speaker's favorite food. In prompted conditions, participants were asked to make the typical truth-lie judgment for each question. In the unprompted condition, they were asked to write down what they thought about the answer. In this condition the researcher was looking for whether participants indicated that the statement was a lie. The prompted and unprompted conditions were conducted as a within-participants variable such that each participant completed both tasks. In the prompted condition, Clare and Levine found the typical results that there was a truth bias, but this bias varied by plausibility. Thus, people were less likely to indicate that implausible deceptions were truths. This demonstrates that there are limits to the truth bias such that deceptions must be plausible for people to believe that they are true.

Interestingly, a different pattern of results emerged in the unprompted conditions in the Clare and Levine (2019) study. These open-ended responses were coded for any mentions of veracity—whether honesty or deception. For participants who completed the unprompted measure first, without mention of the truth-lie judgment, they mentioned veracity in only 4.3 percent of the messages. However, when participants were presented with the prompted measure before the unprompted measure, they mentioned veracity or truth almost 40 percent of the time. Plausibility still had an effect, but the effect was smaller than it was in the prompted conditions. Overall, participants were more likely to make judgments about deception when they were prompted. Without prompting, thoughts about honesty and deception occurred very infrequently, which is consistent with the idea of the truth bias—when hearing statements, people do not even consider the possibility that it could be a lie.

Depending on one's relationship with the communicator of a statement, the truth bias can be increased based on the trust one has with the communicator. McCornack and Parks (1986) examined the truth bias among romantic partners, specifically hypothesizing that greater trust between romantic partners would lead to a higher truth bias and less ability to detect deception from a partner. To test this hypothesis, noncohabitating heterosexual couples were recruited to take part in a deception detection experiment. One partner (the true participant) was randomly assigned to judge the veracity of the statements while the other partner (assigned to be the confederate) produced deceptions. The confederate then filled out an attitude questionnaire in which they were asked to answer half of the questions honestly and the other half dishonestly. The confederates were not fed specific answers but were told only to ensure that the answer was dishonest. The true participant partner had to determine which responses were true and which were lies. Even though participants were told that the statements could be true or false, they tended to believe that their partner was telling the truth at very high rates. Participants judged almost 70 percent of the statements that their partner made as truthful.[2] Furthermore, as people became more confident in their ability to detect deception, they became less likely to presume that their partner was not truthful. Thus, even people who know each other well fall prey to the truth bias.

There are several explanations for why the truth bias occurs (see Vrij, 2008, for a review). Covering all of the explanations is outside the scope of this chapter, but we review two that were alluded to previously in the chapter: the double standard model (Bond & DePaulo, 2006) and truth-default theory (TDT; Levine, 2014). The double standard model can be thought of as a behavioral model because it involves interpreting the behavior of the person communicating the message, whereas TDT can be thought of as a heuristic model (i.e., fast, intuitive judgments that require little cognitive effort). The double standard model argues that people do not like the idea of being lied to and believe that those who are trying to deceive them must be morally bereft and full of shame. Therefore, they believe that deceivers will display nervous behaviors as a manifestation of their shame. However, this idea is problematic because most people do not fit this stereotype and are not morally tormented by lying. Liars often do not display the nervous behaviors stereotypically associated with shame and regret. Because the torment caused by deception resides only in the mind of the person judging the veracity of the statement, and the deceiver displays no notable nervous behaviors, lies are mistakenly thought to be truths.

In our view, Levine's TDT offers a more parsimonious view of the truth bias and truth default than the double standard model. TDT, discussed further in chapter 5, proposes that individuals initially evaluate all incoming messages as honest unless something causes them to suspect that a message is deceptive (Levine, 2014). This truth bias can lead to faulty veracity assessments when an individual who is truth-biased (like most people) encounters a deceptive message but does not doubt the truth of the message. The truth bias may explain why jailhouse informants like Hollman in the Flowers case are so persuasive: people/jurors fall prey to the truth bias and accept what they are hearing is the truth.

Laypeople's and Experts' Stereotypes about Deception

In a perfect world, every person could expertly and accurately determine when someone was lying. This situation would lead to no risk associated with jailhouse informant testimony because jurors would never be fooled by a jailhouse informant's lies. Moreover, prosecutors would interview potential witnesses and automatically exclude those that were untruthful from testifying. Unfortunately, the world is not like that at all, and it is difficult to determine when people are being deceptive. Telling truth from lies is made more difficult by inaccurate beliefs that most laypeople hold about which nonverbal behaviors indicate deception (DePaulo et al., 2003)—and some people, including some jailhouse informants, are skilled liars.

Regarding physiological and behavioral markers of deception, one might believe that certain behaviors associated with increased emotion (e.g., fidgeting or pacing) would be associated with lying. However, as alluded to in the double standard model (Bond & DePaulo, 2006) these behavioral signs can be misleading. When people become emotionally aroused, the autonomic nervous system is initiated, which kick-starts a series of physiological responses such as increased blood pressure, dilated pupils, quickening of the heart rate, etc. It is fair to say that these behaviors can indeed be associated with the arousal caused by deception. However, these responses are not only associated with deceptive behavior, but are also associated with all physical arousal. Thus, they do not reliably predict deception, but only predict physical arousal, which can be caused by a wide variety of stimuli (see DePaulo et al., 2003). For example, it is very difficult to determine if an increase in heartbeat and blood pressure is due to lying or some other emotionally arousing event. Even though these responses—physiological or behavioral—are nonspecific to lying, many people think they are telltale signs, leading them to perceive truths as lies, or lies as truths.

Although physiological cues are not indicative of lying, many laypeople and professionals still believe that physiological cues such as heart rate and dilated pupils are telltale signs of lying (see Vrij, 2008). In terms of assessing people's beliefs about cues to deceptions, there are three methodologies that social science researchers have implemented: surveys, field-based research, and experiments. First, in the survey method, participants are typically given a list of behaviors (e.g., not making eye contact, sweating, fidgeting) and are asked to indicate which of these behaviors are indicative of deception. A survey has the advantage of being easier to distribute, and researchers can sample a broader range of people, making the results more generalizable. The ease of survey administration, however, is offset by the lack of the control given by the experimental method—manipulating one or more independent variables and measuring one or more dependent variables. Second, in field-based research actual real-life statements are analyzed for veracity (see Mann et al., 2004). Thus, these studies offer a greater understanding of real-life situations in which professional lie catchers operate (i.e., determining if a person is lying could result in arrest or incarceration). Because of this, Mann et al. (2004) argue that field studies might be the only valid way to investigate people's actual ability to detect deceit.

Finally, in a lab-based context, researchers have strict control over which individuals are randomly placed into experimental conditions and can eliminate all nuisance variables. Additionally, because a survey lacks experimental control, there is no allowance for drawing conclusions about causal relationships among variables, making survey results largely correlational. Deception research using the experimental method typically requires participants to watch an interview of truth tellers or liars (independent variable) and rate the veracity of the interviewees (dependent variable). The participants are asked to make truth-lie decisions and then are questioned about what led them to their decisions. Often, the interviews are of confederates pretending to lie, and other times they are actual participants who were required to witness something and then told to lie about it (Vrij, 2008). This methodology allows a researcher to assess participants' accuracy in their veracity judgments as well as to analyze their rationale for these judgments.

Research Using the Survey Approach

Survey research on people's perceived cues to deception has been conducted on student populations as well as on police officers (Akehurst et al., 1996). The latter are presumed to be "professional deception detectors" because of their job and training. Across many studies and samples, the results are remarkably consistent (see Granhag & Vrij, 2005, for a review). Both students and police officers stated that decreased eye contact and increased body movement (e.g., fidgeting, postural shifting) are markers of deception. In one study, British police officers were asked how they could tell that someone was being deceptive (Mann et al., 2004). The most frequent response was that liars avert their eyes, and the second most frequent response was body movements (Mann et al., 2004). Neither eye contact nor body movements, however, reliably predict deception (DePaulo et al., 2003).

Although both police and laypeople have incorrect beliefs regarding which cues are indicative of lying, one group that seems to have more accurate beliefs are—fittingly—criminals. As might be imagined, there are not many studies that have examined a criminal sample in the context of a deception detection study (Granhag et al., 2004; Vrij & Semin, 1996). However, the results of these studies are extremely interesting. Granhag et al. surveyed college students, prison personnel, and prison inmates about which cues were indicative of deception. All groups believed that true statements were more consistent than false statements, but prison inmates expressed a greater belief than students or prison personnel. Furthermore, the inmates and officers were less likely to believe that body movements were indicative of lying. The criminals were more knowledgeable about deception, as true statements are not, in fact, more consistent than fabricated statements (Strömwall & Granhag, 2003), and body movements are not a reliable indicator of lying (Vrij, 2000).

In general, subjective behavior cues (e.g., eye contact, body movement) that most people mistakenly believe are indicative of lying are in fact associated with nervousness. It seems that people believe that lying makes the deceiver nervous, causing the deceiver to exhibit certain nervous behaviors. These behaviors include more speech hesitations, frequent pauses while speaking, posture adjustments, and foot movements, as well as less direct eye contact (Vrij, 2000; Vrij & Semin, 1996). Relying on nervous behaviors has been referred to as the "Othello error" (Ekman, 1985, 2001; Vrij et al., 2010). In Shakespeare's play *Othello*, the title character accuses his wife Desdemona of being unfaithful, which causes her to react with a wild emotional outburst. Othello misinterprets the outburst as evidence of Desdemona's guilt.

Perceived cues to deception appear universal. An international research team, called the Global Deception Research Team (2006), conducted a study that included researchers from nearly sixty countries, who surveyed forty participants (twenty males and twenty females) from their respective countries to answer the question, "How do you know when someone is lying?" The modal response was failure to maintain eye contact in 51 of the 58 countries, and it was noted by 64 percent of the participants. The team also found that the participants believed that there were some verbal cues to lying—that liars provide less detail and are less consistent over time. In terms of these verbal indicators, there is more empirical support that these cues may be indicative of lying (Bond & DePaulo, 2006).

As noted earlier, survey research has limitations that complicate the interpretation of the results. One issue with interpretation of the survey responses, as noted by Hartwig and Bond (2011), is that people are notoriously unaware of the basis on which they make their decisions (see Fiske & Taylor, 2008). For example, people often say things like, "I know that he is lying, but I can't tell you how I know; I just do." People may believe that they are being deceived but cannot explain how they know or why they arrived at this conclusion. It is quite possible that participants are unaware of the basis on which veracity judgments are made. Therefore, in survey research, participants may also endorse some cues they believe are indicative of deception, but when questioned further they may reveal that those cues were not the same ones they used when making their actual decision. In a series of four meta-analyses, Hartwig and Bond confirmed their hypothesis that the cues that correlate with deception detection are different from those that people predominantly endorse as indicative in the surveys. In other words, although people report some cues like averting one's gaze as being indicative of lying, they use other cues to make veracity decisions.

Research Using the Field-Based Approach

In a field experiment, actual real-life statements are analyzed for veracity (see Mann et al., 2004). For example, Mann et al. (2004) showed police officers video clips of suspects from actual interrogations. There are two methodological problems with these types of field experiments. First, it is harder to establish the truth of the statements and therefore determine the accuracy of the participants' veracity judgments. The researchers attempt to circumvent this problem by evaluating independent sources of evidence about the statements of the suspects in the videos, such as other eyewitnesses or forensic evidence. However, eyewitnesses are not always reliable and independent evidence does not always exist. Second, as mentioned by Mann et al. (2004), once one finds real-life statements that are verified to be true or false, it is difficult to find true and false statements that are comparable in terms of length, detail, topic, and so forth. However, it might also be that the differences that one finds between real-life true and false statements might themselves be important to research about distinguishing truth from lies. Thus, although it is much harder to establish truth in these field experiments, they afford more ecological validity.

Research Using a Lab-Based Approach

In the lab-based approach, confederates are provided (by a researcher) with truthful or deceptive statements about their attitudes or behaviors. These statements are then given to participants, who must decide if each statement is true or false. Often, participants are also asked to describe how they arrive at these decisions (Vrij, 2008). One advantage of the laboratory approach is that the researcher always knows whether a statement is true or false.

An example of using the laboratory approach to show participants' inability to detect lies comes from the false confession literature (Kassin et al., 2005). Kassin et al. videotaped ten prisoners giving both true and false confessions. For the truthful conditions the inmates confessed to the crime they committed, and for the deception conditions they confessed to a crime committed by another inmate in the study. These videotaped interviews were then shown to college students and police officers who were asked to make veracity judgments (i.e., which confessions were true and which were lies). The police officers were no more accurate than college students in identifying the true and false confessions. In fact, both groups' accuracy rates were not significantly different from chance.

Similar results were found in a study by Mann et al. (2004) that employed real-life materials in a field study. Mann et al. asked police officers to detect deception from parts of videotaped interviews of actual suspects. These suspects were chosen because their statements were either verified or proven false by evidence such as reliable statements by independent witnesses and forensic evidence. If a case was included, only those clips in which each word was known to be a truth or a lie were presented to the participants.

Along with their veracity judgments, the police officers were also asked to justify their choice by indicating which specific behaviors they relied on. In this study, the accuracy rate was slightly higher than chance, but the two behaviors most relied on were eye gaze and body movement. Unfortunately, there is little to no empirical support for these police officers' beliefs (Granhag & Vrij, 2005). As noted earlier, DePaulo et al. (2003) concluded that eye contact was a weak or inconsistent indicator at best, and Strömwall et al. (2004) found that fidgeting, frequent posture shifts, and grooming were not indicative of lying.

As with the survey research, criminals tend to be good at detecting deception in lab-based settings. In a laboratory study, Hartwig et al. (2004) had college students and prison inmates make veracity judgments of videotaped statements of witnesses telling either the truth or a lie about an event. College students performed at chance (57 percent), but inmates performed significantly above chance (65 percent). Participants were also asked to indicate which information they used to make their veracity judgments. After making their veracity judgments, participants were asked to give a justification for their decision in their own words. Interestingly, the most frequent justification from inmates was the plausibility of the statement. In other words, inmates often responded that a statement was a lie because it was just implausible. The research validated the inmates' belief as implausibility has been shown to correlate with deception (DePaulo et al., 2003). College students, on the other hand, most often indicated consistency throughout the statement as the basis of their judgments. In fact, although truth tellers provide more detailed accounts, their stories are not more consistent over repeated accounts (see Vrij et al., 2010, for a review).

A possible concern with the studies mentioned so far is that most, if not all, of the studies involved people lying about issues that have no impact on their life. Liars might be more convincing and harder to detect if being caught had serious negative consequences—what are referred to as high-stakes lies. Only a handful of studies have examined lie detection with high-stakes lies (see Vrij et al., 2010). In one of these studies, Vrij and Mann (2001) presented Dutch police officers with videotapes of press conferences in which family members of a murder victim asked the public for help in finding the murderer. All the people speaking in the press conferences were known to have lied because they had subsequently been convicted for the murder for which they were asking the public for help. These crimes had taken place in England and were shown to the Dutch police officers to avoid the possibility that the participants were aware of the outcome of the case. As is typically found with lies that are not high stakes, these police officers still performed at chance levels in their veracity judgments of high-stakes lies. Thus, even with trained police officers and liars who are motivated to appear truthful due to the high stakes associated with the lie, accuracy rates were no better than guessing (but see Ekman et al., 1999, for contrasting results with police officers, judges, FBI agents, and forensic psychiatrists).

Further Challenges in Detecting Deception

Vrij et al. (2010) have catalogued a series of what they refer to as "pitfalls" to detecting deception. It is not our aim to review all the pitfalls in this chapter, but three of them seem particularly relevant to the task of jurors confronted with jailhouse informant testimony: (a) lies that are rehearsed or practiced, (b) lies that are embedded in truths, and (c) overconfidence in one's ability to detect lies.

Detecting deception becomes even more difficult when the deceiver has practiced the deception, which is something that individuals have been shown to do (Hartwig et al., 2007). A consistent finding from deception research is that liars are known to prepare answers in anticipation of an interview (Hartwig et al., 2007). Like most witnesses, jailhouse informants may rehearse their stories in anticipation of contacting law enforcement officials or testifying in court. It is likely that, in preparation for testimony, they also go over their testimony with their lawyers. This preparation may make lies more difficult to detect because prepared lies display fewer cues to deception than spontaneous lies (DePaulo et al., 2003). However, the benefits of rehearsing a lie (i.e., making it difficult for others to detect deception) can occur only if the liars know or anticipate specific questions that will be asked. In the case of trial testimony, it is almost a certainty that jailhouse informants will be able to anticipate questions in advance. Like other witnesses, jailhouse informants will have been prepared by the prosecution—rehearsing responses to direct examination and cross-examination questions. Because the testimony was rehearsed, it may be difficult for jurors to determine whether a jailhouse informant's testimony was true or false.

The task of detecting liars is made even more difficult, according to Vrij et al. (2015), by the fact that lies are often embedded in truthful accounts. Liars will often tell stories that are mostly true and change specific but vital details. This is often true of jailhouse informants, whose testimony generally matches the evidence of the case (see Neuschatz et al., 2020). To the extent that the testimony matches the evidence in the case, jailhouse informants may only be lying about how they acquired the information, not about the facts of a crime. There is evidence that embedding lies within the truth is common among criminals (Hartwig et al., 2007; Vrij et al., 2015). Vrij et al. (2010) speculated that effective liars are likely to be people that do not find lying cognitively challenging and do not experience guilt or fear when lying—and these are typically characteristics of jailhouse informants.

Another factor that inhibits accurate detection of deception is that people are overconfident in their ability to detect liars (Vrij et al., 2010). People believe that they are better at identifying liars than they truly are. This is true of both laypeople and professionals (Vrij et al., 2010). Police are more confident than students in their ability to detect lies, but they are not more accurate (DePaulo & Pfeifer, 1986; Kassin et al., 2005). This overconfidence is also present in other professional groups, such as FBI and CIA agents (Allwood & Granhag, 1999). This may create a problem, especially in the courtroom, when there is a jailhouse informant. To the extent that jurors believe that they and the police are skilled at detecting lies, they may mistakenly but confidently believe the testimony of the jailhouse informant and give more weight to the testimony, even though it may be false.

Jurors and Jailhouse Informants

It should be clear from the foregoing discussion that there are several impediments to detecting liars like Hallmon, the jailhouse informant. Most important in this regard is that people tend to have a truth bias, so they are not actively scrutinizing messages for deception. Instead, they assume that messages are true unless they are otherwise persuaded (Levine, 2014). Not only do both laypeople and police have a bias toward believing that messages are true, but they also rely on cues that are not correlated with lying. However, there are no verbal or nonverbal cues that are uniquely related to lying (see DePaulo et al., 2003). This makes jurors' task of detecting deception from jailhouse informants extremely daunting.

The prevalence of wrongful convictions due to jailhouse informant testimony is evidence of the difficulty of detecting deception for jurors. For instance, jurors who believe that prosecutors vet the veracity of a witness's statement before allowing them to take the stand would not expect a prosecution jailhouse informant to lie. These beliefs, as well as pro-prosecution biases, likely increase the perceived credibility of prosecution witnesses, including jailhouse informants. In this way, jailhouse informants may benefit from increased credibility due to what some legal experts have termed "implicit prosecutorial vouching" (Covey, 2014; Roth, 2016; Wetmore, Neuschatz, Roth, et al., 2020). Jurors may assume that the mere fact that the prosecution has allowed the jailhouse informant to take the stand is evidence of truthful testimony. The idea of implicit prosecutorial vouching is supported by studies suggesting that jurors attribute inflated credibility to expert witnesses testifying on behalf of the prosecution because jurors consider them to have passed the judge's standards of proof (Cutler et al., 1989; Schweitzer & Saks, 2009). Because of this view, jurors may remain in the truth-default state and may fail to recognize, or may simply dismiss, evidence of deception within the jailhouse informant's testimony. Jurors may believe that the jailhouse informant's statements are, as the jailhouse informants often claim, the "honest" truth. Or jurors may simply attribute any possible signs of deception (inconsistency) to a nondeceptive reason (nerves) (DeLoach et al., 2020).

Summary

Research on deception makes clear why a jailhouse informant, such as Hallmon, presented at the start of the chapter, would still be believed by jurors despite his stating at his second trial that he lied on the witness stand. Individuals (a) have a bias to believe that others are truthful (Levine, 2014), (b) are inaccurate at detecting deception (Vrij, 2008), and (c) rely on the wrong nonverbal cues when making truth judgments (see DePaulo et al., 2003). When one couples these three findings with the fact that many people have an implicit belief that a prosecutor has vetted her witnesses and would not let a dishonest person testify, the task of detecting falsehoods from a jailhouse informant becomes extremely difficult.

In the next chapter, we turn to the perception of jailhouse informants in court.

5

Perceptions of Jailhouse Informants in the Courtroom

Clarence James Dailey was convicted of the murder of fourteen-year-old Shelly Boggio in 1985. Dailey remains on death row today. His legal team maintains that there is no evidence connecting Dailey to the crime: no eyewitnesses and no physical or forensic evidence. In fact, the codefendant in the case, Jack Pearcy, who was also convicted of murdering Boggio and was Dailey's housemate at the time of the murder, signed a declaration that he alone killed Shelly. The major evidence linking Dailey to the crime was a jailhouse informant named Paul Skalnik. As outlined in detail by Colloff (2019), Skalnik was a career con man and jailhouse informant and was doing time for grand theft auto at the time of Dailey's trial. Skalnik had a long criminal history—he served as witness for the prosecution in thirty-five different cases, sending at least three people to death row (see Colloff, 2019, for a full account of Skalnik's history).

On May 5, 1985, Boggio, her sister, and a friend were picked up near St. Petersburg, Florida, by Pearcy and Dailey. The two men brought the girls back to their place, where they proceeded to get high and drink beer. According to Dailey, later that night he, his girlfriend, and Pearcy dropped off Boggio's sister and friend. Then the four, including Boggio, went to a local bar. After leaving the bar, according to Dailey, they went back to their house and Pearcy dropped off Dailey and his girlfriend. Pearcy then agreed to go out again to take a friend who was in the house, Shaw, to a pay phone and bring Boggio. Dailey insists that he went to sleep in the house while Pearcy took Shelly home. After making the phone call, Shaw walked back to the house while Pearcy left with Boggio. There is a phone record that shows Shaw made the call around one fifteen in the morning, and the medical examiner put the time of

Boggio's death at between one thirty and one forty-five. When Pearcy got back around four o'clock in the morning, he woke up Dailey and they smoked more marijuana. Then they played frisbee, and Dailey insists that he retrieved an errant throw from the water and got his pants wet. Later that day, Boggio's body was found in a causeway near St. Petersburg (Colloff, 2019).

At trial, the prosecutors called three jailhouse informants, all of whom were in jail with Dailey as he was awaiting trial. All three testified that Dailey confessed to them. The third of these jailhouse informants was Paul Skalnik. During Dailey's trial Skalnik testified that Dailey confessed to him, and on the stand Skalnik offered vivid details about the murder and the knife that was used to kill Boggio. Dailey maintains that he never talked to Skalnik, although several weeks before the trial Dailey said he was moved to the same wing in the jail as Skalnik. According to Skalnik, Dailey confessed to him through his jail cell as Skalnik was in the hallway (Colloff, 2019).

Informants and jailhouse informants are a well-established feature of the American criminal justice system (*Hoffa v. US*, 1966; *US v. Ford*, 1878). Although prevalent, the use of jailhouse informants can be dangerous, as false testimony from jailhouse informant witnesses is a leading factor in wrongful convictions (Garrett, 2011). Unfortunately, precise statistics on informant use at the state and federal levels are unavailable for a variety of reasons. For example, if there is a plea deal before the trial, then information regarding the informant is not preserved. Furthermore, many states do not retain information on who has testified as a jailhouse informant—and attempting to find that information by examining trial transcripts is a daunting, arguably impossible task. In the US federal system, however, it is estimated that approximately 10 to 12 percent of defendants have their prison sentences reduced each year in exchange for their cooperation with the government (Roth, 2016; US Sentencing Commission, 2017). Since 2005, one out of every eight convicts (approximately 48,895) in the federal prison system has had their prison sentences reduced by up to ten years in exchange for helping government investigators (Heath, 2012). Jailhouse informants are also widely used at the state level, but similar statistics are generally not recorded (but see Roth, 2016; Virginia Criminal Sentencing Commission, 2018). Despite the widespread use of jailhouse informants, their use is largely unregulated; and (as has been noted in other chapters) jailhouse informant testimony has even contributed to wrongful convictions.

One major reason that prosecutors continue to use jailhouse informant testimony at both the state and federal levels is because of the persuasive quality of jailhouse informant testimony. But why are jailhouse informants serving as witnesses in court—why are those who have already committed or are suspected of committing crimes, sometimes many crimes, such influential witnesses? We begin by describing the common characteristics of jailhouse informants and discuss a survey of laypeople and lawyers regarding opinions about jailhouse informants. Last, we discuss what the psychological literature can tell us about this form of testimony, including the content and persuasive qualities of informant testimony and the typical informant's motivation for testifying. There are three aspects of psychological research pertaining to jailhouse informants that we discuss: (a) laypersons' and lawyers' opinions of jailhouse informant testimony, (b) laboratory research investigating the impact of jailhouse informants on legal decision making, and (c) theoretical explanations as to why jailhouse informant testimony is so persuasive.

Survey Research: Laypersons' and Lawyers' Opinions

Given that testimony from disreputable jailhouse informants like Edward Fink can lead to wrongful convictions or, in the case of Thomas Thompson (*People v. Thompson*, 1988), an execution, it is important to understand how jurors perceive jailhouse informant testimony. This is especially vital considering that the US Supreme Court has long recognized the prejudicial and unreliable nature of jailhouse informant testimony—but has opined that there are safeguards within the judicial system that protect the rights of the accused. For example, any deal brokered with a jailhouse informant must be disclosed to the defense (e.g., *Giglio v. US*, 1972; *US v. Singleton*, 1998). However, it is less clear how secondary confessions, or statements from a jailhouse informant, are perceived in the courtroom.

To better understand the perception of jailhouse informant testimony, Key et al. (2018) conducted a survey of university students, community members, and defense attorneys.[1] Participants were asked to rate several types of evidence—DNA, eyewitness testimony, fingerprints, confessions, other forensic evidence, secondary confessions, and character witnesses—in terms of which evidence was most believable. Although the groups differed in their overall rankings, all three groups rated secondary confessions as the second least believable type of evidence, just above character witnesses. Additionally, there was almost no difference in the beliefs of the two lay groups (students and community members). Specifically, the survey results revealed, among other things, that:

- Only 14 percent of the college sample and 13 percent of the community members agreed that jailhouse informant testimony should be permissible if the jailhouse informant had committed a crime of deceit (i.e., perjury or fraud)
- Over 50 percent of college students (59.6 percent) and community members (53.6 percent) indicated that the jailhouse informant should be allowed to testify
- Only 38.3 percent of defense attorneys believed that jailhouse informants should be allowed to testify in general
- About 40 percent of the lay sample (college students 40.3 percent and community members 43.62 percent) agreed that law enforcement should be allowed to offer incentives, such as reduced jail time, in exchange for a secondary confession

- Over 80 percent of the sample agreed that the jury should be informed that the jailhouse informant was receiving an incentive for their testimony (college students 84.2 percent and community members 84 percent)
- Around 70 percent of the lay sample and nearly all defense attorneys (90 percent) thought that the jury should also be informed if the jailhouse informant had previously testified in the same capacity for the prosecution in other trials

In addition to the above results, the data indicated that although the college and community participants understood the factors that influenced the reliability of secondary confessions, they still underestimated how this testimony affects jurors:

- Only slightly more than one-fourth of the respondents believed that a secondary confession from a jailhouse informant would be persuasive to jurors (college students 30.4 percent and community members 28 percent)
- When there was no incentive offered in exchange for the secondary confession, around 40 percent of the community (37.6 percent) and student (41.5 percent) samples indicated that the jury would vote guilty based on this testimony
- Slightly more than half of the defense attorneys (57.5 percent) believed that the juries would render guilty verdicts when there was no incentive
- When the jailhouse informant was offered an incentive, only 18.4 percent and 20.5 percent of students and community members believed that the jury would vote guilty; however, 44.6 percent of defense attorneys believed that the jury would vote guilty even after being informed that the jailhouse informant was receiving an incentive to testify

The Impact of Jailhouse Informant Testimony on Legal Decision Making

It is clear from the exoneration cases discussed earlier in this book that testimony from jailhouse informants is extremely persuasive. Moreover, psychological research using mock trial studies (most often using murder trials) finds that jailhouse informant testimony is so compelling that mock jurors often inappropriately give more weight to jailhouse informant statements when deciding on a verdict, leading to an increase in guilty verdicts (Neuschatz et al., 2008). Additional research has shown that mock jurors' inability to properly evaluate informant testimony occurs even when jurors are presented with evidence that should cast doubt on an informant's reliability (e.g., being told that the jailhouse informant received an incentive). For example, Neuschatz et al. (2008, Experiment 1) investigated the impact of incentive disclosure during the cross-examination portion of the informant's testimony. Participants read a trial transcript that either included a secondary confession from a jailhouse informant or did not include a secondary confession (i.e., a control condition). For those who read a transcript in which a jailhouse informant testified, the researchers manipulated whether the jailhouse informant's testimony stated that he was receiving an incentive—five years off his prison sentence—in exchange for testifying. Upon completion of the trial, participants rendered a verdict and rated the informant's interest in truth, his trustworthiness, his interest in justice, and his own self-interests. The results indicated that mock juror participants voted guilty more often when the jailhouse informant testified compared to when he did not testify. Regarding the incentive manipulation, mentioning an incentive did not impact verdicts, but the participants did believe that a jailhouse informant who received an incentive was less interested in serving justice and more interested in his own self-interests. These results suggest that although mock jurors recognized that the informant was selfishly motivated and uninterested in justice, they were unable to consider the information they received about the jailhouse informant's incentive and entertain the possibility that his testimony was unreliable.

Neuschatz et al.'s (2008) finding that mock jurors did not consider the incentive a jailhouse informant receives when weighting the value of his testimony must be discussed further, given psychological research on motivation and incentives. Deception detection research has demonstrated that people lie to achieve some desired goal that they cannot achieve through more honest methods (Levine et al., 2010). Jailhouse informants are no exception, as those who testify are often promised a reward (through incentives) and are willing to fabricate their testimony to receive it. This is especially true if an incentive is quite large. Keep in mind that although incentives usually come in the form of a reduced prison sentence or dropped charges (Garrett, 2011), there can also be smaller inducements, such as money, cigarettes, or privileges while in prison (Neuschatz et al., 2008). As stated by the US Court of Appeals Fifth Circuit in *US v. Cervantes-Pacheco* (1987), "It is difficult to imagine a greater motivation to lie than the inducement of a reduced sentence, but courts uniformly hold that such a witness may testify so long as the government's bargain with him is fully ventilated so that a jury can evaluate his credibility" (p. 315). In the section that follows, we discuss why people lie and how even small incentives can entice people to do so.

People's goal in a situation is critical for whether they will decide to lie. Specifically, it has been found that people generally choose to lie when it provides the easiest route in attaining their goals (Levine et al., 2010). Levine et al. suggest that people will opt to be truthful as opposed to lying if they can still accomplish their goals with the truth. In three studies, Levine et al. (2010) tested the hypothesis that people are more likely to lie when the truth is problematic to their goals. Participants were asked what they would say in six situations about different topics: (a) a gift, (b) a friend's body weight, (c) a friend's cooking, (d) a date, (e) a movie opinion, and (f) a favor to go to the post office. Motive to deceive was manipulated by using two different versions of the situation. For example, in the situation involving the friend's cooking, all participants were asked how they enjoyed the food while learning that the host had spent the entire day preparing the food. In the deceptive-motive condition, the participants were told that they hated the food, but in the no-motive condition they were told that they loved the food. All participants were then given a two-alternative forced-choice test in which they had to respond whether they either liked or disliked the food.

When there was no motive to deceive, participants chose the honest answer, that they enjoyed the food. However, when the food was not to their liking, 62.5 percent of participants chose the dishonest answer indicating that they liked the food; not everyone in this condition chose the dishonest response. Levine et al. (2010) indicated that people were more likely to lie when telling the truth was incompatible with their goal of being a good friend. By contrast, people are unlikely to be deceptive when their goal can be achieved by being honest.

Although incentives motivate people to lie, their influence is not considered by mock jurors (Neuschatz et al., 2008). These incentives do not have to be as large as getting out of jail. Indeed, incentives that are relatively small can lead individuals to lie. One study compared high school students from a private religious school and a public school to see if they would cheat (Bruggeman & Hart, 1996). Students were asked to complete a circle test (see Hartshorne & May, 1928) that requires participants to memorize the position of ten circles on a piece of paper, then close their eyes and place a number label (1–10) on their respective circles. After completing five trials, participants recorded the number of circles that they correctly placed on the corresponding numbers. Bruggeman and Hart (1996) told participants that they could receive extra credit on their final grade if they performed well on the circle test. More specifically, they were told that the average score for high school students was 27 correct circles over the course of five trials. Participants reported their own scores, and the circle test sheets were anonymized so that participants' responses could not be verified. A control group, unaware of any opportunity for extra credit, was used to establish a baseline score of 10.67 correct. Any student that reported a 22, or three standard deviations above the control scores, was classified as a liar. It is of course true that some people could just have outstanding memories and accurately remembered more than 22 items correctly on the circle test. However, the number of people in the population whose memory is better than three standard deviations above the mean, or over the 99th percentile, is likely to be small in any study, including this one, and probably would have little effect on the results.

The results from Bruggeman and Hart (1996) found that about 75 percent of participants lied about their performance (total number of circles successfully labeled) in hopes of gaining a small amount of academic credit. The results did not vary with high school type—as students in both the religious (70 percent) and public (79 percent) school lied at about the same rate. These results suggest that people will lie for even a minimal incentive. It is important to note that these are high school students lying to receive academic credit, not incarcerated individuals who have broken the law and may be highly motivated by the promise of getting closer to freedom.

It is not just the incentive but the incentive coupled with the likelihood of being caught that motivates people to lie (Kajackaite & Gneezy, 2017). To test this, Kajackaite and Gneezy used a cheating game in which participants were told to roll a six-sided die in private and then report the results to the experimenter. Participants were told that if they rolled a particular number (e.g., 5) then they would receive a monetary payoff. However, rolling any other number (i.e., 1, 2, 3, 4, or 6) would result in no payoff. Incentive was manipulated by varying the amount of money that participants would receive for rolling a 5 ($X = $1, $5, $20, and $50). With a fair die, a 5 (or any number) should be rolled at rate of one-sixth, or 16.7 percent. The authors hypothesized that if incentive influenced lying, then participants in the higher incentive conditions ($20 and $50) would report rolling a 5 significantly more often than 16.7 percent of the time, whereas participants in the lower incentive conditions ($1 and $5) would report rolling a 5 around 16.7 percent. The results revealed that the rate of rolling a 5 was not significantly different from chance (16.7 percent) in any condition. Thus, increasing the incentive did not increase lying. The authors argued that lying is also influenced by the probability of being caught. The reason that lying did not increase with incentive, according to the authors, is that as incentive goes up, so does the fear of being caught.

Kajackaite and Gneezy (2017) suggested that lying follows a cost-benefit analysis; once the incentives are deemed to be higher than the cost, people will lie. In the context of jailhouse informants, these results indicate the possibility that jailhouse informants will be more likely to lie, as the incentive is greater than the punishment for lying. More specifically, if there is *no* cost or punishment for getting caught, then the incentive for a jailhouse informant will always be higher than the cost. Thus, there is no real reason for jailhouse informants not to lie on the witness stand—note that to our knowledge, it is very rare for a jailhouse informant to be charged with perjury for lying (see Natapoff, 2009).

The fact that the cost-benefit analysis for jailhouse informants favors lying (enormous benefits like getting reduced jail time without any costs—no risk of punishment) becomes increasingly concerning when one considers the magnitude of false secondary confession evidence. Research has identified the high likelihood that jailhouse informants will provide false secondary confessions, even in a trivial situation with a meager incentive. Swanner et al. (2010) investigated the factors that would convince participants to provide a false secondary confession by adapting a paradigm that was found to prompt individuals to provide false primary confessions (Kassin & Kiechel, 1996). To accomplish this, pairs of participants were informed that they would be working together on a typing task, but the participant who had been assigned to be the typist must be sure to avoid pressing the tab key, as it would cause the computer to crash. Regardless of what keys the participant pressed, the computer was programmed to crash after one minute. Both the typist and reader were individually asked to inform the experimenter of what happened. The results not only corroborated previous findings, in that the typists frequently provided false primary confessions, but also exposed a propensity for participants to provide false secondary confessions (i.e., reporting that the typist caused the computer to crash).

A more recent investigation of participants' willingness to perjure themselves for an incentive was conducted by Robertson and Winkelman (2017). In this study, participants were presented with a vignette that instructed them to assume the role of a prisoner facing charges for a minor felony. Specifically, the participants were told that they were charged with tax evasion and were facing a maximum sentence of three years in prison and up to $270,000 in fines and fees. Participants were also told that while they were in custody they were to be placed next to another inmate's cell and that they were going to be questioned by detectives about the fellow inmate's guilt in a murder case. Finally, the participants were informed that the authorities had evidence against the other inmate but that they needed to ensure the conviction in the other inmate's case. The participants were then randomly assigned to one of two conditions: (a) informed that they did in fact hear the defendant confess with specific details (truth condition) or (b) informed that the inmate was an elderly man who was an alcoholic (false condition). Participants were then presented with increasing levels of incentives, ranging from a reduced maximum sentence from three years to two years (level 1) to the offer of complete immunity as well as financial support throughout the duration of the trial (level 4). Overall, it was found that 7 percent of participants were willing to lie in exchange for the lowest incentive level. As one can imagine, the number of participants willing to fabricate evidence increased as the incentive level increased. At level 4, 20 percent of the participants indicated that they would be willing to lie.

In a follow-up experiment, participants imagined themselves in a situation of being prosecuted if they did not testify against a defendant (Robertson & Winkelman, 2017; Experiment 2). In this experiment, participants were asked to testify against a state governor who was accused of appointing a company CEO in exchange for a monetary bribe—this information was false. Thus, participants were placed in the position of facing prosecution if they did not testify against the defendant, despite the knowledge that what they were testifying to would be false information. The participants were offered either probation or outright immunity in exchange for their testimony. Additionally, half of the participants were told that whatever incentive they were receiving would be disclosed to the jury during trial. Overall, more than half (55 percent) of participants were willing to testify despite the knowledge that they would be committing perjury. It is important to note that the participants had nothing to gain in real life by lying. For this reason, it may be that the number of participants willing to lie in both experiments likely underestimates the number of jailhouse informants willing to lie and falsify evidence because jailhouse informants are actual prisoners offered the opportunity to ease their own burdens.

The above research on incentives demonstrated that people were willing to lie for minimal benefits (Bruggeman & Hart, 1996; Swanner et al., 2010) and that their willingness to lie increased with the size of the incentive (Gneezy et al., 2013). This is particularly disconcerting when applied to jailhouse informants, given that social-psychological research is conducted, for the most part, with college students and community members who are not imprisoned and who most likely have never been in trouble with the law. If these law-abiding people will lie for as little as credit on a final grade (Bruggeman & Hart, 1996), credit in a psychological experiment (Swanner et al., 2010), or a small monetary reward (Gneezy et al., 2013; Kajackaite & Gneezy, 2017) or even in an imagined situation in which there is no true danger posed (Robertson & Winkelman, 2017), then one can imagine that the temptation to lie would be even stronger for individuals looking to gain freedom. The findings from these social-psychological research studies are consistent with archival analyses on these points. For example, the Los Angeles County Grand Jury (1990) report specifically stated that incentives provide jailhouse informants motivation to fabricate testimony.

Imagine what someone who has already broken the laws of society and is incarcerated will do for a large incentive such as time off their prison sentence. Jailhouse informants are, for the most part, practiced liars, and the incentive offered to them can be relatively large (see *US v. Cervantes-Pacheco*, 1987). The results described above are particularly concerning when one considers that there is virtually no cost to a jailhouse informant for lying, as they are almost never prosecuted for perjury (Natapoff, 2009). This may be the result of the legal system perpetuating practices in which incentives offered to jailhouse informants outweigh the cost of lying—which means jailhouse informants can fabricate evidence with relative impunity.

The above research makes clear that individuals (including jailhouse informants) were motivated to lie to receive an incentive. However, this motivation did not appear to be acknowledged by those judging a court case—that is, by jurors. For example, Neuschatz et al. (2008) interpreted their findings (i.e., participants used jailhouse informant testimony when rendering a verdict) in terms of fundamental attribution error (FAE; Ross, 1977). As a reminder, FAE involves participants attributing the jailhouse informant's willingness to testify due to dispositional factors (e.g., the jailhouse informant's personality led him to do the right thing—testify) and underestimating the situational factor of the incentive. To further explore FAE when jailhouse informants testify, Neuschatz et al. (2008, Experiment 2) conducted a follow-up study using the same methodology, but this time asked participants why they believed that the jailhouse informant came forward to testify. Most participants believed that the informant decided to testify because of dispositional factors (e.g., he felt guilty or was sorry for the family) instead of situational factors (e.g., the incentive of a sentence reduction). This finding offered clear support for the interpretation that mock jurors succumbed to FAE. Instead of acknowledging the powerful nature of an incentive in getting a jailhouse informant to testify, participants believed that the jailhouse informant was motivated to testify by a moral imperative (i.e., a dispositional attribution).

Further research on the impact of jailhouse informants has investigated whether secondary confessions were as compelling as other types of evidence (e.g., primary confessions). In Experiment 1 by Wetmore et al. (2014), participants were presented with a trial summary that contained a secondary confession, eyewitness testimony, and character testimony. After reading the trial summaries, participants made verdict decisions and then ranked the probative value of all four forms of evidence. Consistent with the primary confession literature, participants who voted guilty ranked the secondary confession to be the most incriminating piece of evidence (Kassin & Neumann, 1997). Wetmore et al. replicated these results in Experiment 2.

Wetmore et al. (2014, Experiment 3) conducted an additional study to directly compare the power of primary versus secondary confessions. Participants read four different trials, for murder, assault, rape, and theft, and each trial contained a crucial piece of evidence—a primary confession, secondary confession, or eyewitness testimony. There was also a no-evidence control condition for each type of trial. When presented with any type of confession evidence—primary or secondary—participants voted guilty more often than when they were presented with the eyewitness testimony or with the control condition across three of the four trial summaries (all except the rape trial).

Although Wetmore et al. (2014) did not find an impact of jailhouse informant testimony in the rape trial, more recent research extended the generalizability of the impact of jailhouse informant testimony to the context of child sexual assault and adult acquaintance rape. In two experiments, Golding et al. (2020) found that jailhouse informant testimony increased guilty verdicts and pro-victim ratings (i.e., victim credibility) across both child and adult victims, and across male and female victims. Golding et al. noted that the differences in results from Wetmore et al. (2014) may be due to the short nature of the trials and that Wetmore et al. included an adult stranger rape scenario—a less common rape scenario in real life. It should also be noted that Golding et al. used Pathfinder analyses to show that mock jurors' representations of the trials highlighted the importance of jailhouse informant testimony when presented.

The preceding research indicated the impact (e.g., increased guilty verdicts) that jailhouse informant testimony had in a variety of cases. Additional research showed that jailhouse informant testimony not only influences jurors' verdicts but also has a corruptive influence over other forms of evidence. For instance, research showed that jailhouse informants can influence eyewitness identifications (Mote et al., 2018). In this study, participants viewed a video of an armed robbery. They then identified a suspect from a photo array and reported their confidence in that decision. Next, participants received a police report that contained confirming information, disconfirming information, or no feedback regarding their identification decision. In the confirming feedback condition, participants were told that the person that they identified had confessed or had been implicated by a jailhouse informant. In the disconfirming feedback condition, participants were led to believe that they chose the wrong person; more specifically, participants were told that there was an individual in the lineup—but not the one that the participant had chosen—that either had implicated himself (e.g., disconfirming primary confession) or was implicated by the jailhouse informant (e.g., disconfirming secondary confession). Additionally, there was a disconfirming feedback denial condition in which participants were told that although they identified the suspect, he denied being the culprit of the crime. Once participants had received the feedback, they again reported their identification confidence; they could change their identification decision or maintain their initial decision before rating their confidence again.

The results from Mote et al. (2018) indicated that evidence provided by jailhouse informants contaminated eyewitness identifications. Of participants who made an initial identification (choosers), 80 percent of those who received the disconfirming feedback via evidence from the jailhouse informant (the disconfirming secondary confession condition) later identified a different lineup member. Mote et al. highlighted that the choosers were twenty times more likely to change their identification decision relative to the participants in the no-feedback condition. A corresponding effect was found for participants who did not make an initial identification (non-choosers); 52 percent of non-choosers later identified a lineup member after receiving disconfirming feedback wherein the jailhouse informant implicated one of the lineup members. These findings are consistent with the primary confession literature, which has found that confession evidence has the capability to influence eyewitnesses (Hasel & Kassin, 2009).

Other research also demonstrated that the corruptive influence of jailhouse informant testimony has a broader impact on other types of forensic evidence. Jenkins et al. (in press) investigated whether a secondary confession from a jailhouse informant contaminated the evidentiary independence of handwriting evidence. In this study, participants were presented a case summary that briefly described a bank robbery: the culprit demanded money from the teller by handing her a note with the words, "I have a gun. Keep quiet or I will shoot you. Give me all your cash!" The summary further stated that a suspect was apprehended and positively identified by the teller. Participants were then told that the suspect signed a handwritten Miranda Rights waiver (*Miranda v. Arizona*, 1966) before an interrogation. Participants then read either statements from a jailhouse informant (depicted as reliable or unreliable) or statements from the suspect himself, who had confessed but recanted. The informant reported that the suspect had confessed his guilt to him; the suspect either confessed but later recanted or maintained his innocence throughout the interrogation (the latter two conditions were control conditions).

Participants in Jenkins et al. (in press) were then presented handwriting evidence of the signed Miranda Rights waiver (*Miranda v. Arizona*, 1966) along with the bank robbery note. The robbery note handwriting samples were manipulated such that they either matched the Miranda waiver or did not match (mismatch condition). Following this, participants were asked to judge the similarity of the handwriting samples and to render a verdict decision. Participants who read a confession from a reliable jailhouse informant rated the handwriting samples higher in similarity (40 percent) and were more likely to vote guilty (39 percent) compared to those who read a confession from an unreliable jailhouse informant (21 percent and 23 percent for match and guilt, respectively). Furthermore, the percentage of handwriting-match judgments for the participants who read the secondary confession from the reliable jailhouse informant (40 percent) and for the participants in the recanted primary confession condition (43 percent) were similar. These results demonstrated that, as established in the primary confession research, secondary confessions can contaminate and influence the interpretation of mock jurors' evaluations of forensic evidence such as handwriting evidence (Kukucka & Kassin, 2014).

Theoretical Perspectives on the Persuasiveness of Jailhouse Informant Testimony

As described above, mock jurors continue to trust and believe jailhouse informant statements (Neuschatz et al., 2008). We discuss four theoretical explanations for why this occurs.

Fundamental Attribution Error (FAE)

As noted earlier, Neuschatz et al. (2008) interpreted their finding that mock jurors unreasonably used jailhouse informant testimony in terms of FAE. When jurors commit FAE in the context of jailhouse informants, they believe that the informant came forward because of moral reasoning (e.g., doing the right thing) rather than because of selfish reasons (e.g., a sentence reduction). One study investigated this issue more closely by examining whether the lack of effect of jurors' knowing about incentives received by the jailhouse informant on verdict decisions was due to FAE. Specifically, participants read a criminal trial summary with one of three types of informant witnesses (accomplice, jailhouse informant, or a community member) who either received an incentive (five years off their sentence or ten thousand dollars if they were a community member) or did not receive an incentive (Neuschatz et al., 2008, Experiment 2). Participants were asked in an open-ended question about why they believed that the informant decided to come forward and testify. These responses were then coded as dispositional (e.g., he felt bad for the victim's family), situational (e.g., he was receiving an incentive), both, or neither. Overall, 75.32 percent of participants believed that the jailhouse informant came forward due to dispositional or personal factors, whereas only 15 percent believed that the jailhouse informant came forward due to situational factors.

Later studies showed similar findings about FAE (Neuschatz et al., 2012; Wetmore et al., 2014). Neuschatz et al. (2012) used the same materials as Neuschatz et al. (2008), with the only difference being that Neuschatz et al. (2012) added the testimony history of the jailhouse informant (Experiment 1). Specifically, participants were told that the jailhouse informant had testified zero, five, or twenty times in the past as a jailhouse informant and that they either were or were not getting an incentive. In this study, although neither testimony history nor knowledge of an incentive affected verdict decisions, 84 percent of participants attributed the cooperating witness's motivation for coming forward to dispositional factors (Neuschatz et al., 2012, Experiment 1). Additionally, Wetmore et al. (2014; Experiment 2) found that 57 percent of participants named dispositional rather than situational reasons for the informant coming forward. While this number is lower than in previous studies (Neuschatz et al., 2008; Neuschatz et al., 2012), the percentage of dispositional motives provided was significantly higher than the percentage of situational motives provided. It seemed that regardless of whether the jailhouse informant was receiving getting an incentive, participants fell prey to FAE and that information such as incentive presence will not mitigate the misguided trust placed in the jailhouse informant's testimony.

Truth-Default Theory (TDT)

Another possible theoretical explanation for why jurors use jailhouse informant testimony can be found in TDT (Levine, 2014; as suggested by DeLoach et al., 2020). As stated earlier, TDT stipulates that people generally exist in a constant state of truth bias. This is because most of the interactions people experience *are* truthful. This bias allows for more effective and efficient communication between people (Levine, 2014). In the setting of a courtroom, however, TDT may be problematic. For instance, most people tend to continue to exhibit a truth bias in the courtroom. Levine (2014) states that unless a statement includes deceptive intent, awareness, or purpose, it is considered the truth. It seems that unless sufficient evidence is provided suggesting that someone is lying, people automatically believe that a person in court is telling the truth. Therefore, jurors are prone to believe witnesses, even those with questionable reliability such as jailhouse informants, unless evidence is provided to suggest that a jailhouse informant is lying. If, however, adequate evidence that a statement may be a lie is provided, the receiver of the statement's message may leave the truth-default state and move into a state of suspicion. For this series of events to happen, a trigger event is required to cause feelings of wariness. An example of a trigger event is when the receiver of a message learns that the sender is motivated to deceive by reasons such as an ulterior motive or an incentive (Reeder et al., 2004). Given a trigger, the message receiver temporarily exits the truth-default state and begins evaluating the veracity of the statement. If enough evidence is provided and a threshold is overcome, active judgments of honesty are made (Levine, 2014). However, if the threshold is not crossed, the message receiver may return to their original truth-default state. The illumination of any potential motivations (e.g., the jailhouse informant explicitly reveals why they are testifying) may provide jurors with adequate suspicion to abandon the truth-default state and enter a state of determining deception (DeLoach et al., 2020). If the defense can draw out the motivations of the informant for testifying, jurors may cross the suspicion threshold and doubt the veracity of the testimony.

Tunnel Vision

Another reason jailhouse informant testimony can have such detrimental effects in the courtroom is tunnel vision—a group of logical errors and heuristics (Findley, 2012). Heuristics are informal guidelines as opposed to formal rules (Ashcraft, 2006) and can be thought of as cognitive rules of thumb. However, while heuristics can lead to the correct decision, they will not guarantee an accurate decision every time. Two heuristics that affect legal decision making are "belief preservation" and "confirmation bias." Belief preservation refers to the fact that people have a natural tendency to maintain a belief, even when confronted with evidence that the belief is no longer valid. Confirmation bias refers to the tendency of people to seek out evidence that is consistent with their conclusions and to discredit or discount evidence that contradicts their conclusions (Findley & Scott, 2006). We should note that prosecutorial vouching can be thought of as a form of confirmation bias. It occurs when people believe that any witnesses brought forth by the prosecution have been properly vetted and meet the judge's standards of credibility (Roth, 2016). This assumption often leads jurors to automatically accept a witness's testimony, in this case that of a jailhouse informant, as true without searching efficiently for any evidence that the witness's statement is untrue. With these heuristics at hand, one can see the ease with which a jailhouse informant will be viewed as reliable and trustworthy.

The inclination for people to hold onto beliefs and conclusions even in the face of disconfirming evidence (i.e., belief preservation) has been supported in the lab (Nickerson, 1998). For example, Ross et al. (1975) had participants judge the authenticity of suicide notes. During the task, participants were given feedback about their performance. This feedback consisted of being told that they were achieving either below- or above-average accuracy. However, the feedback was randomly determined and was not related to performance at all; after completing the experiment, participants were informed that the feedback was fake. Even after being told that the feedback was not related to performance, participants who received positive feedback rated their own performance higher than people who were given negative feedback. Thus, they were unable to discount fictional information and as a result maintained their belief in their ability to judge the veracity of suicide notes.

It is easy to see how heuristics can affect jurors' ability to accurately assess the reliability of jailhouse informants. As previously mentioned, in their archival study of DNA exonerations, Neuschatz et al. (2020) found that jailhouse informants made many statements that were inconsistent with case facts or with statements that they had previously given. The belief preservation heuristic may explain why jurors still voted guilty even after they learned about the jailhouse informants' inaccuracy. Despite being exposed to cross-examination and the impeachment of the jailhouse informant, the jurors clung to their belief that the informant was truthful. These results are similar to those found by Ross et al. (1975), wherein the participants continued to believe that they were skilled in detecting the accuracy of suicide notes even when they were told that the feedback they received was false.

The other heuristic noted earlier, confirmation bias, can also explain why jurors tend to believe the testimony of jailhouse informants. Confirmation bias is the tendency to interpret evidence in line with one's existing beliefs while ignoring evidence that does not align with beliefs (Findley & Scott, 2006). A classic example of confirmation bias is the Wason Four Card Problem (Wason, 1966). In this problem, participants are presented with four cards that have a letter on one side and a number on the other side. For example, participants might be presented with the cards showing the letters E and K and the numbers 4 and 7. The participants' task is to test the rule that any card with a vowel on one side has an even number on the reverse side. The most common responses were to turn over the cards with the E and 4. Flipping the E card confirmed the rule. The problem is that turning over the 4 card offers no relevant information because if there is a consonant on the other side, it does not violate the rule that cards with a vowel have an even number on the other side.

To adequately test the rule, participants would have to turn over the 7 card. If the card with the 7 facing up has a vowel on the other side, then the rule is disconfirmed. Overall, only 4 percent of Wason's participants correctly chose to turn over the 7 card. To test any rule, one needs to determine situations that violate it. This is known as the "falsification principle." As evidenced by the fact that only 4 percent of participants used the falsification principle, most people have the tendency to avoid disconfirming evidence. In other words, 96 percent of participants demonstrated the confirmation bias. Thus, to the extent that jurors believe that an informant is telling the truth, they will accept the testimony, discount any inconsistencies in their testimony, and avoid searching for any evidence of deception.

A form of confirmation bias in court occurs with the previously discussed phenomenon of prosecutorial vouching. Individuals believe that prosecutors have a duty and responsibility to present the truth and therefore have properly vetted all witnesses (including jailhouse informants) before allowing them to testify (Roth, 2016). In other words, there is a general feeling among jurors that prosecutors have done their due diligence, have verified the accuracy of the testimony before trial, and would not let an unreliable witness take the stand. When jurors rely on prosecutorial vouching, they by extension tend to exhibit a pro-prosecution bias. If jurors have a pro-prosecution bias and evaluate subsequent evidence in a manner that coincides with that existing bias, they are also falling prey to the confirmation bias. As jailhouse informants provide information that fits the fact pattern that has been presented by the prosecution, some jurors may discount inconsistencies in a jailhouse informant's testimony because this testimony also contains specific details of the crime that match those of the prosecution's argument. Thus, jailhouse informant testimony may be persuasive to jurors because it conforms to the jurors' preconceived notions about the prosecution. In addition, evidence that is at odds with jurors' biases toward the prosecution is discounted or interpreted in a way that is consistent with the jurors' biases. For example, any inconsistent statements may be deemed as irrelevant or easily explained away (e.g., "perhaps the informant simply just forgot") (see Cutler et al., 2014, for a review of confirmation bias as it applies to primary confessions).

Story Model

During a trial, jurors are active participants. They process and organize evidence into a narrative or story. This story, according to the story model (Pennington & Hastie, 1986, 1988, 1993), explains the case "facts," ultimately leading jurors to a verdict. Note, however, that given that evidence is presented by opposing sides, the prosecution and the defense, jurors may need to develop more than one story during a trial. Research by Pennington and Hastie showed that participants (a) considered evidence stronger when it was presented as a story instead of on a witness-by-witness basis and (b) prefer a story format. In addition, Groscup and Tallon (2016) found that the strength of one story relative to another story has the greatest impact on the verdict rendered.

As to what makes one story stronger than another, the story model maintains that each story's coverage, coherence, and plausibility are considered by jurors. Regarding coverage, jurors determine how well each piece of evidence fits into the story. As more evidence is integrated into a particular story, the story's coverage is greater, thereby increasing jurors' confidence in a particular narrative as the "correct" story (Groscup & Tallon, 2016). Next, coherence is the overall logic of a story; it has three components: consistency, completeness, and plausibility. Stories that are consistent have few (if any) pieces of evidence that conflict with one another. Complete stories do not have any gaps; all the evidence needed for a causal explanation of what happened is present. Finally, a plausible story makes sense in terms of jurors' understanding of how the "real world" works (Devine, 2012). Note that plausibility is likely grounded in one's knowledge and beliefs about the world.

We argue that the story model can explain the impact of jailhouse informants on jurors. To begin, jailhouse informant testimony is typically presented in murder and rape trials, in which the evidence is often circumstantial, and the verdict usually hinges on contradictory stories. During a trial, a jailhouse informant testifies that the defendant confessed to committing a crime. This critical piece of evidence is integrated into jurors' prosecution story about the case, thus strengthening the story. The defense tries to present evidence that leads to the construction of another strong story (i.e., the defense story). However, the strength of the defense story is negatively impacted by the defense typically being unable to counter the jailhouse informant's testimony, even if it was false. This inability to counter the jailhouse informant is magnified by the defendant usually not testifying. Ultimately, the construction of these two stories is a guilty verdict.

Summary

There are several conclusions that can be drawn from the research on mock jurors' perceptions of jailhouse informants. First, based on the survey results by Key et al. (2018), students and community members understand the problems with jailhouse informant testimony but underestimate the influence that this testimony has on them. Second, even small incentives can motivate people to lie (Bruggeman & Hart, 1996) when there is very little possibility of getting caught or if the punishment for being caught is trivial (Kajackaite & Gneezy, 2017). Third, although there is a large motivation for jailhouse informants to lie, this does not seem to lessen their impact on the verdicts of mock jurors or actual jurors. In the laboratory, it is consistently found that jailhouse informant testimony significantly increases guilty verdicts (Neuschatz et al., 2008; Neuschatz et al., 2012; Wetmore et al., 2014) compared to when this testimony is not presented. For real-life jurors, the impact of jailhouse informants is evidenced by the relatively large number of DNA exonerations in which the original conviction involved false secondary confessions from jailhouse informants (Neuschatz et al., 2020). Finally, the undue weight given to jailhouse informants can be attributed to several possibilities. These include jurors committing the fundamental attribution error (FAE). In other words, jurors often attribute the motivations of jailhouse informants to dispositional factors (e.g., jailhouse informants want to see justice for the family or victim) as opposed to the situation (e.g., jailhouse informants are getting a benefit for their testimony). Another possibility is that the persuasiveness of jailhouse informant testimony could be attributed to TDT or prosecutorial "vouching." In the case of TDT, jurors may simply have not crossed the threshold of suspicion to doubt the veracity of jailhouse informants. Prosecutorial vouching may work hand in hand with TDT, as the jurors may not be suspicious of jailhouse informants' testimony because they trust that the prosecutor has already verified it. Thus, the jurors have no reason to doubt the veracity. Regardless of which theory is correct, jailhouse informants make very believable witnesses. We turn next to research examining potential safeguards against false testimony from jailhouse informants.

6

Expert Testimony, Cross-Examination, and Judicial Instructions

On May 29, 1996, fifteen-year-old April Pennington snuck out of her parents' house to meet P. J. Allain for the purpose of smoking marijuana and having sex. After Pennington left her house and met up with Allain, they were picked up by George Leniart, and the three of them drove to a secluded area. The three drank beer and smoked marijuana, and then Leniart allegedly took Allain aside and said he wanted to have sex with Pennington. Allain, according to his own account, immediately informed Pennington that Leniart intended to rape her. Pennington asked to have intercourse only with Allain, which she did, as Leniart watched through the windshield of a car. After Pennington and Allain had sex, Leniart raped Pennington. Leniart then took Allain home, and after that drove Pennington to an unknown location in the woods where she was eventually killed. At Leniart's trial, the prosecution contended that Leniart admitted to four individuals, each on separate occasions, to killing Pennington. The four people were Allain and three inmates—Michael Douton, Zee Ching, and Kenneth Buckingham. Leniart was incarcerated with these three inmates while he was in jail for the sexual assault of a different victim—a thirteen-year-old girl. In 2010, Leniart was convicted of Pennington's murder and sentenced to life in prison based, in part, on the testimony of the cooperating witnesses.

The story did not end there. In 2019, the Connecticut Supreme Court overturned Leniart's convictions and granted him a new trial. The court agreed with the defendant's argument that the case against him depended heavily upon the testimony of the three jailhouse informants. The informants corroborated Allain's story, which, according to the court, was the critical evidence in the case. Furthermore, the prosecution conceded that the secondary confessions from all the informants differed about several details of the event. The court argued that the defendant should have been allowed to present expert testimony to the jury concerning the general unreliability of jailhouse informant testimony. Interestingly, it was noted in the appeal that the judge in the original trial excluded an interview with Allain. In this interview, the interviewing officer reminded Allain that it would be in his best interest to cooperate with the state in securing a conviction against Leniart because he would receive favorable treatment and likely avoid any criminal charges himself. Note that this deal was being offered to a man who, if his own story is to be believed, stood by while Pennington was raped. This decision by the Connecticut Supreme Court was very important because experts on cooperating witnesses and jailhouse informants have had difficulty being admitted to testify even though all defendants have the right to expert testimony, and cases that include jailhouse informants are no exception (*State v. Leniart*, 2020).

Much of the difficulty revolving around experts testifying in cases with jailhouse informant testimony is the result of a ruling by the US Supreme Court in *Hoffa v. US* (1966; see chapter 2). In this case, the court ruled that although informant testimony may be unreliable, "the established safeguards of the Anglo-American legal system leave the veracity of a witness to be tested by cross-examination, and the credibility of his testimony to be determined by a properly instructed jury" (p. 311). In addition to cross-examination of a jailhouse informant and instructions to jurors about the reliability of a jailhouse informant's testimony, legal safeguards include requiring prosecutors to disclose any incentives that informants receive for testifying (*Brady v. Maryland*, 1963; see chapter 2) and allowing defense attorneys the possibility of introducing expert testimony (*State v. Leniart*, 2020). The growing number of overturned convictions based on unreliable secondary confessions from jailhouse informants that have been presented throughout our book, however, demonstrate that jurors are often persuaded by jailhouse informants and that the proposed safeguards may be inadequate at mitigating their impact.

In the discussion that follows, we review three judicial safeguards that are meant to protect the accused against unreliable or prejudicial evidence: expert testimony, cross-examination, and judicial instructions. We acknowledge that there are other safeguards such as pretrial reliability hearings as well as opening and closing arguments, but there is only limited research on these topics from which to draw meaningful conclusions. In what follows, we examine the efficacy, from a psychological point of view, of each judicial safeguard. Finally, we conclude the chapter by evaluating whether these judicial safeguards are a viable way to inform juries about the dangers of jailhouse informant testimony.

Expert Psychological Testimony

The legal standard for admitting scientific evidence (including expert testimony) was established in *Frye v. US* (1923). The resulting Frye Rule required evidence to be generally accepted in the relevant scientific field for it to be admitted into evidence. The Frye Rule was later replaced by another US Supreme Court ruling, *Daubert v. Merrell Dow Pharmaceuticals* (1993). In this later case, the US Supreme Court ruled that the Federal Rules of Evidence (adopted by Congress in 1975) superseded *Frye v. US*. The new standard was based on Rule 702 of the Federal Rules of Evidence (Ala. R. Evid. 702, 1975), which stated that judges would now be the gatekeepers for scientific expert testimony. With the Frye Rule, judges were not the gatekeepers and had to defer to the relevant community of experts to answer the key question of whether the scientific evidence in question is generally accepted in the field. In addition, *Daubert v. Merrell Dow Pharmaceuticals*, unlike *Frye v. US*, applies to all expert testimony, whereas *Frye v. US* applies only to scientific evidence. Under *Daubert v. Merrell Dow Pharmaceuticals*, judges would now determine if an expert could testify based on (a) if the expert testimony is relevant to the case and helpful to the triers of fact (that is, the jury) and (b) if the conclusions given by the expert testimony were reliable and derived from scientific knowledge. These standards and other rules of the Federal Rules of Evidence have shaped federal and state standards on the admissibility of experts. Thirty-four states have adopted court rules that attempt to codify the law of evidence in accordance with the Federal Rules of Evidence (Graham, 1989).

Since the fourteenth century, the courts have sought the knowledge of experts to assist and educate jurors (Wigmore, 1904). However, the admission of psychological experts in court (including in jailhouse informant cases) can be controversial (Melton et al., 2007). Typically, in cases involving jailhouse informants, experts are excluded from testifying for two general reasons. First, it is felt that the research the expert would testify about (e.g., deception) is not sufficiently advanced to reach the admissibility threshold. Second, a judge may feel that the expert's information would not aid the jurors and instead might confuse them (Cutler & Kovera, 2011). Before they are possibly excluded, experts are initially subjected to a *Daubert* (*Daubert v. Merrell Dow Pharmaceuticals*, 1993) or reliability hearing.[1] It is interesting to note in this regard that jailhouse informants can testify in almost every state without any reliability hearing or evidence corroborating their testimony.

There are two reasons to expect that jurors in cases involving jailhouse informants would benefit from expert testimony about psychology. First, as we have pointed out several times in this book, there is a link between wrongful convictions and false testimony from jailhouse informants (see Garrett, 2011). This is especially true in rape and murder cases where the evidence is generally weak or circumstantial (see archival analysis by Neuschatz et al., 2020). As mentioned in the introduction, false testimony from jailhouse informants is one of the leading causes of wrongful convictions in capital cases (Warden, 2004). Gross et al.'s (2005) analysis of the 340 DNA exoneration cases studied from 1989 to 2003 found that 97 of these cases included some sort of perjury—much of which came from cooperating witnesses, which included jailhouse informants. Furthermore, false testimony from jailhouse informants was a contributing cause to wrongful convictions in 56 percent of murder cases and 25 percent of rape cases. Clearly, as mentioned in chapter 5, jurors have difficulty detecting when others are being deceptive. Second, not only do people have trouble detecting deception, but they are also unaware about the dangers of testimony from jailhouse informants (i.e., that it may be false; Garrett, 2011; Key et al., 2018). Thus, it appears that an expert could assist the trier of fact regarding some of the misperceptions of jailhouse informant testimony.

Although psychological expert testimony might be useful for jurors in a case involving a jailhouse informant, an expert must also prove to a judge that the evidence they will provide is reliable based on *Daubert v. Merrell Dow Pharmaceuticals* (1993). The determination of evidence as reliable is the sole decision of the judge; there are no formal criteria. However, based on *Daubert v. Merrell Dow Pharmaceuticals*, the US Supreme Court has listed four nonexhaustive factors that judges can consult to decide the reliability of an expert: (a) Can the data be falsified? (b) Have the data been subjected to peer review or publication? (c) Are there known or potential error rates? and (d) What is the general acceptance of the findings in the relevant scientific community? This is not meant to be an exhaustive list, and the US Supreme Court recognized that there is no set of guidelines that could adequately capture a definitive test of all the different types of technical and scientific evidence that a court might be exposed to.

We now discuss each factor cited in the *Daubert v. Merrell Dow Pharmaceuticals* (1993) decision. The first factor is falsifiability. Scientifically, falsifiability refers to the ability of a scientific statement to be tested and disproved by empirical evidence (i.e., compared to a comparison group). An expert can certainly say, based on experimental data, that people will produce false secondary confessions even with minimal incentives (Swanner et al., 2010). In addition to the research, there is a growing body of DNA exonerations that support the conclusion that jailhouse informants can and do give false testimony (Garrett, 2011; Neuschatz et al., 2020). Can a psychological expert say for certain, however, what the base rate of a jailhouse informant's lying is? The answer is no. There are no data on true secondary confessions because there is simply no way to calculate their rate. Even when there is inculpatory DNA evidence, this does not confirm the veracity of the secondary confession.

Regarding the second *Daubert v. Merrell Dow Pharmaceuticals* (1993) factor of peer review, there is now a growing body of peer-reviewed jailhouse informant literature. In addition, there is a considerable literature on jailhouse informants in law reviews and legal journals. While typically not peer reviewed before publication, law reviews serve the important function of bringing specific empirical findings to the legal community and can allow for legal scholars to critique scientific research.[2] Legal scholars can judge the relative importance of the peer-reviewed research for legal settings. There is also a considerable literature on false confessions, jury decision making, and social influence in various disciplines (e.g., psychology, sociology, communications, etc.), all of which an expert on jailhouse informant testimony could draw upon to form their opinion.

The third *Daubert v. Merrell Dow Pharmaceuticals* (1993) factor of evaluating expert testimony concerns the known error rate. Regarding a known error rate for jailhouse informant testimony, things get a bit tricky because this point typically means different things for social scientists and legal professionals. The known error rate for social scientific research is by convention set at .05 or .01. These numbers represent the probability that the results in the experiment are due to chance and not due to the experimental manipulation. In other words, if the error rate is set at .05, a researcher would expect the result fewer than five times in one hundred to be due to chance variation (e.g., biased sampling, experimenter error, individual differences, and so forth) and not an experimental manipulation. As scientists, we are willing to accept these error rates, but these are not the error rates the courts are looking for. Judges want to know the likelihood that the jailhouse informant is lying and the error rate associated with the opinion that the jailhouse informant is lying. In simpler terms, if there are ten jailhouse informants, how many of them are lying? In addition, what is the margin of error in that estimate? How likely is it that the estimate is wrong? Given the nature of social science research, an expert would not be able to answer those questions from a judge. The best that an expert can do is to outline factors that are present in jailhouse informant testimony and factors that may be typical to false confessions. For example, an expert might state that statements from a jailhouse informant that are inconsistent with the case facts are typically a risk factor for false testimony. The expert might also say that if two statements are inconsistent, then one of the statements must be wrong, but the expert could not say which one is wrong. The expert could not state with confidence that because a jailhouse informant made an inconsistent statement, the informant must be lying about everything.

The inability of an expert to make a definitive statement in the above example reflects how social scientific research makes general statements that apply to most, but not all, individuals. Social scientists make predictions about the average, or most typical, behaviors of a population, not single members of the population. Because of this way of thinking, it is difficult (and probably inappropriate) for social scientific experts to make definitive statements about the accuracy of any witness. This probabilistic way of thinking is very different from that of the law, which is more case specific (see Brigham, 1999).

There is relatively little disagreement among psychologists about the reality of false jailhouse confessions; the relevant scientific community accepts these findings, which is the fourth factor in *Daubert v. Merrell Dow Pharmaceuticals* (1993). It is also accepted that false secondary confessions from jailhouse informants are a contributing factor to wrongful convictions (see Wetmore, Neuschatz, Roth, et al., 2020). We have not seen one commentator, lawyer, judge, or social scientist argue that false secondary confessions do not occur. Some may argue that not all of them are false and that jailhouse informants are valuable to the legal system, but they acknowledge that false secondary confessions exist. In addition, there are no disagreements that certain psychological tactics increase the risk of false secondary confessions (see Neuschatz et al., 2020).

There have only been two published studies investigating the impact of expert testimony on jailhouse informant testimony (Maeder & Pica, 2014; Neuschatz et al., 2012). The two studies used very different types of experts. In the first study, Neuschatz et al. (2012) attempted to reduce the fundamental attribution error (FAE) in jurors by educating them on the ease by which inmates could obtain inculpatory information that could be included in their false secondary confessions. As a reminder, the FAE is the tendency for people to make dispositional attributions as opposed to situational attributions (Ross, 1977). As applied to jurors in cases with jailhouse informants, it would mean that jurors would believe that informants were testifying because they wanted to do the right thing or felt bad for the victim's family (dispositional attribution) as opposed to because they were receiving some type of benefit for their testimony (situational attribution).

Neuschatz et al. (2012) had student participants read a mock trial in which a jailhouse informant testified for the prosecution and a former jailhouse informant (i.e., an expert) testified for the defense. A control condition had no expert. The expert was described as a former criminal who had himself given testimony as a jailhouse informant many times in the past. Although such a person is not a traditional expert, he passes the expert witness criteria under *Daubert v. Merrell Dow Pharmaceuticals* (1993). According to these criteria, an expert is someone who has knowledge, based on extensive previous experience or study, that a juror may not have. In this study, the expert had no effect on mock jurors' verdict decisions as they voted guilty equally as often in the expert and no-expert conditions. Interestingly, the expert also had no effect on participants' ratings of the credibility of the prosecution's jailhouse informant. Hearing the expert testify about the ease with which evidence can be obtained in jail had no effect on participants' attributions about the jailhouse witness's trustworthiness, truthfulness, or interest in justice. Thus, learning from an expert about how easy it is to obtain information in jail did not reduce guilty verdicts or affect mock jurors' impressions of the informant.

The use of a scientific expert on jailhouse informants was also equally ineffective at reducing guilty verdicts in another study conducted by Maeder and Pica (2014). These researchers had community members read the same trial used in the Neuschatz et al. (2012) study but had a scientific expert (as opposed to a former jailhouse informant) testify for the defense—there was also a no-jailhouse-informant control condition and a no-expert control condition. The expert was a social scientist who testified about how jurors, according to the research, were insensitive to the fact that incentives can induce people to lie and how FAE affects jurors. In addition, the expert testified that false jailhouse informant testimony was one of the leading causes of wrongful convictions in capital cases. Finally, the authors varied the size of the jailhouse informant's benefit for testifying: no incentive, small (sentence reduction of six months), medium (sentence reduction of one year), or large (sentence reduction of two years).

As is typically found in jailhouse informant research, guilty verdicts were highest in the conditions where the mock jurors read the testimony of a jailhouse informant as opposed to the conditions where they did not. Guilty verdicts when a jailhouse informant testified did not vary with expert testimony. The guilty verdict rates were similar in all conditions regardless of whether there was an expert or not. Having an expert testify about the effect of incentives did not even reduce guilty verdicts in the conditions where the jailhouse informant testified that he was receiving an incentive. Although incentive size influenced participants' perceptions of the informant—participants felt more positively toward the jailhouse informant when there was no incentive as opposed to when there was one—incentive size did not interact with their perceptions of the expert.

The above two studies (Maeder & Pica, 2014; Neuschatz et al., 2012) on the use of expert testimony in jailhouse informant cases would seem to indicate that such testimony will not be effective as a safeguard against false jailhouse informant testimony. There are, however, several reasons to cast doubt on this interpretation. First, it would not be prudent to draw such broad conclusions from only two studies. Clearly, more research is warranted before firm conclusions can be drawn. Second, in the two studies there was no reason given to doubt the veracity of the jailhouse informant. Just because jailhouse informants received an incentive does not mean that they were lying. A more stringent test of expert testimony would be to examine the interaction of the reliability of the jailhouse informant and expert testimony. Research could examine if participants are more likely to believe that a jailhouse informant's testimony was false if two conditions are true: (a) that the informant testimony was inconsistent with the facts (i.e., unreliable) and (b) that an expert testified about the perils of this type of testimony. For example, would an expert be more persuasive if the jailhouse informant's testimony changed from interview to trial? The answer to this question would be yes if the expert could point out that the jailhouse informant's testimony has changed and that the two versions could not both be correct. This would at least give the mock jurors a reason to doubt the testimony, with or without an incentive having been offered to the jailhouse informant. Third, jailhouse-informant-specific experts may be effective because other psychological experts have been shown to be effective in the context of cases involving false confession (Blandón-Gitlin et al., 2011; Cutler & Kovera, 2011). It stands to reason that if experts work in primary confession cases, it is likely that they will be helpful in other situations, including those with a jailhouse informant; both are a type of confession.

Finally, the published studies did not include experts who provided a reason to doubt the jailhouse informant's testimony. For example, in the published studies done to date (Maeder & Pica, 2014; Neuschatz et al., 2012) the informant was offered an incentive; however, an incentive to testify does not in and of itself mean the testimony is false. It means only that the jailhouse informant wanted something for coming forward to testify. Thus, the expert testimony may not have reduced guilty verdicts because the participants were not convinced that the incentive meant that there was deception. A more sensitive experimental design is needed before any conclusions about jailhouse-informant-specific expert witnesses can be properly evaluated.

Regarding the impact of expert testimony in other research domains, researchers have found positive effects of expert psychological testimony on a wide variety of cases (Cutler & Kovera, 2011). These areas include, but are not limited to, false memory ploys (Woody et al., 2018), primary confessions (Blandón-Gitlin et al., 2011), eyewitness testimony (e.g., Cutler at al., 1989), and sexual assault cases (Schuller & Hastings, 1996; see Costanzo et al., 2007). For example, in two experiments, Woody et al. (2018) examined the effects of false evidence ploys and expert testimony on the decision making of judges and mock jurors. A false evidence ploy refers to a method in which the interrogator attempts to get the suspect to confess by telling the suspect that there is evidence linking the suspect to a crime when, in fact, no such evidence exists. In this situation, a police interrogator might tell the suspect to confess because the police found the suspect's fingerprints at the crime, when there, in fact, were no prints at the crime scene.

Participants who were college students (Experiment 1) read a summary of a murder trial (Woody et al., 2018). The experimenter manipulated false evidence ploys (present or absent) and expert testimony (present or absent). In the false evidence ploy condition, participants read that the suspect's denials were confronted with false information—the interrogators claimed that an eyewitness saw the suspect at the victim's residence on the day of the murder. In the expert testimony/false evidence ploy condition, an expert talked about the increased risk of a false confession when such tactics are used. In the expert / no false evidence ploy condition, an expert testified about other interview tactics, such as minimization (downplaying the seriousness of the crime and the penalties) and maximization (exaggerating the strength of the evidence and the punishment associated with the crime), that increase the risk of false confessions. Participants were put in groups of six to eight to deliberate as a jury. The results revealed that a false evidence ploy in police interrogations did not influence verdicts compared to the condition with no false evidence ploy. Expert testimony did, however, have a significant effect. More specifically, expert testimony made it less likely that deliberating juries would convict (16.3 percent guilty) compared to the no-expert condition (34.9 percent guilty).

Not only has expert testimony been shown to sensitize jurors against false evidence ploys, but there is also evidence that such testimony helps jurors become more sensitive to factors that increase the risk of false primary confessions. Blandón-Gitlin et al. (2011) presented college students with a trial transcript where the main piece of evidence in the case was the confession of the defendant, which was disputed on the grounds that it was obtained in a coercive manner. An expert witness for the defense was offered at trial. Participants, both before and after the testimony, made judgments of the defendant's guilt and of the coerciveness of the interrogation tactics. Participants' pre-expert-testimony guilt ratings were significantly higher than their post-expert-testimony ratings (89.7 vs. 76.5 percent). Furthermore, participants rated interrogation tactics as more coercive post–expert testimony than pre–expert testimony.

In addition to their ability to effectively educate jurors, there are several other important reasons why courts should consider using experts in cases that involve jailhouse informants. First, as noted in the survey of laypeople's opinions on jailhouse informants, jurors do not understand the dangers associated with jailhouse informant testimony or the effect that incentives have on behaviors (see Key et al., 2018). Second, jurors over-rely on jailhouse informant testimony (see Wetmore et al., 2014). Wetmore et al. (2014) found that secondary confessions are just as persuasive as primary confessions and are more compelling to jurors than eyewitness testimony. Third, judges and attorneys perceive expert witnesses as useful to a jury under many circumstances, including in cases of false primary confessions (Cutler et al., 2020; Cutler & Kovera, 2011). Fourth, as will be mentioned in the next section, traditional methods of impeaching witnesses, such as cross-examination, are generally not effective with jailhouse informant testimony (see Leippe, 1995). Leippe also argues that lawyers may not be knowledgeable about the relevant issues pertaining to jailhouse informant testimony. To the extent that lawyers are not very knowledgeable about these issues, they cannot ask pertinent questions when cross-examining a jailhouse informant. For example, lawyers may not know about FAE or may be unaware of how a jailhouse informant receiving an incentive can affect jurors' perceptions of the jailhouse informant. An expert can educate these lawyers, judges, and juries about these important issues. In addition, there are some questions that can be answered only by an expert, such as questions about research investigating the effect of an incentive on lying, or whether police and lawyers are able to detect deception better than laypeople. It would likely be useless to ask a jailhouse informant if incentives motivate people to lie or if inconsistent statements are typically associated with false secondary confessions. Only an expert can objectively review the research on these topics, thereby answering these questions and educating the court.

Although jurors' decisions may be influenced by expert testimony, not all agree that social scientists should offer expert testimony (Melton et al., 2007). There is the classic argument (Wigmore, 1970) of whether the findings from controlled laboratory experiments can be generalized to the complexities of real-world events. In other words, do mock jurors reading a trial transcript or watching a mock trial of an expert really put themselves in the position of an actual juror? Scholars have made similar arguments regarding other types of social science experts. For example, does laboratory research on eyewitness memory really capture the combined effects of factors such as stress, exposure time, and retention interval? Can experts really explain how these factors affect the identification of real witnesses (Flowe et al., 2009)? Regarding secondary confession, are those factors that produce real-world secondary confessions the same as those factors that induce false secondary confessions in the laboratory?

Cross-Examination

The legal standard for cross-examination dates back much further than the Frye Rule (*Frye v. US*, 1923). In fact, cross-examination can trace its origins to both Roman law and English common law, which guaranteed the accused the right to look the accuser in the eye (*Coy v. Iowa*, 1988). In the United States, the right to cross-examine a witness derives from the Confrontation Clause in the Sixth Amendment. This amendment specifies that the accused has the right to confront the person or persons bringing charges against them. The US Supreme Court has stated that the "Confrontation Clause guarantees an *opportunity* for effective cross-examination" (see *Delaware v. Fensterer*, 1985).

Regarding cross-examination and jailhouse informants, the US Court of Appeals for the Fourth Circuit established several safeguards that the government is required to follow when a compensated witness is going to testify at trial (see Natapoff, 2009). These safeguards include (a) any compensation arrangement between the prosecution and the informant is disclosed to the defense, (b) jurors need to be instructed that there is an agreement between the witness and the prosecution, and they should consider the implications of the agreement when they consider the testimony, and (c) the defendant can cross-examine the witness (Natapoff, 2009). As mentioned earlier, the US Supreme Court has acknowledged that compensated testimony from jailhouse informants is extremely unreliable; however, the Court also argues that these existing trial mechanisms such as cross-examination are sufficient to protect the accused from a wrongful conviction (*Giglio v. US*, 1972). This argument is based on the notion that jurors will be able to evaluate the truthfulness of an informant's testimony and discount unreliable information with the aid of the safeguards (Covey, 2014). In the following section, we will evaluate the ability of jurors to accurately determine the reliability of jailhouse informant testimony; we will assess whether cross-examination is sufficient in protecting the innocent and in preventing wrongful convictions.

The procedures inherent within cross-examination are thought to be crucial for evaluating the accuracy of evidence as well as for exposing unreliable or dishonest evidence obtained during direct examination (Wheatcroft et al., 2004). In theory, cross-examination should protect the accused by allowing the jury to consider the true motivations of the witness who is testifying (Wheatcroft et al., 2004). Thus, cross-examination is intended to serve as a means for jurors to evaluate the overall credibility of a witness's testimony. Unfortunately, cross-examining jailhouse informants can be very challenging for the defense, especially when a jailhouse informant has been previously coached and prepared by the prosecution. Moreover, a secondary confession made by a jailhouse informant can be difficult to corroborate or contradict—it is the word of a jailhouse informant against the word of a defendant (Natapoff, 2009).

During cross-examination, opposing counsel asks specific questions with the goal of undermining the direct testimony of a witness. For example, the questions may address issues of fact that were omitted during direct examination. Another technique used during cross-examination is to ask leading questions to discredit a witness brought to the stand. Leading questions are those that prompt a particular answer or seek to confirm an answer (*The Law Dictionary*, 2009). These questions generally, but not always, can be answered with a yes or no. For example, "You did not see the stop sign when you drove through it, did you?" This is leading because it assumes the person drove through the stop sign. Leading questions, although not allowed during direct examination, are allowed during cross-examination and can be a very useful and effective method for impeaching a witness. Leading questions are intended to reveal signs of prejudice, incompetence, or dishonesty within a witness's testimony (Kassin et al., 1990). Overall, if used appropriately and astutely, leading questions can be an effective tool for lawyers.

As is the case with expert testimony, research involving cross-examination in the context of jailhouse informant testimony is scarce. DeLoach et al. (2020) examined how cross-examination of jailhouse informants' ulterior motives, inconsistencies in testimony, and alternative explanations for how the informant acquired their information would influence verdict decisions. Undergraduate participants listened to a trial transcript in which a jailhouse informant's testimony was manipulated. During cross-examination, the defense attorney pointed out one of the following or a combination of the three: (a) the jailhouse informant's ulterior motive to provide false testimony, (b) an inconsistency between the informant's testimony and a prior statement made by the same jailhouse informant, and (c) an alternative explanation for how the jailhouse informant learned the privileged or nonpublic crime details. Note that the alternative explanation manipulation consisted of the defense attorney confronting the jailhouse informant with an explanation that the jailhouse informant was told about a nonpublic crime fact (i.e., how the victims were restrained) from a friend who visited him in jail as opposed to being told by the defendant. The friend stated that he learned about the nonpublic crime fact from his girlfriend, who worked in the police department. DeLoach et al. found that cross-examination reduced conviction rates when there was an inconsistency between the jailhouse informant's testimony and when there was an alternative explanation of how he learned about nonpublic details. That is, participants were more likely to convict when the inconsistency was absent (39.2 percent) than when it was present (24.3 percent), and when there was no alternative explanation (36.8 percent) than when there was an alternative explanation (26.7 percent). Cross-examination did not influence participants' guilty verdicts when they were exposed only to the alternative explanation of how the jailhouse informant obtained the information.

Although DeLoach et al. (2020) is the only published study investigating the cross-examination of jailhouse informants, research on eyewitness memory has also shown that cross-examination of witnesses' inconsistent statements influences mock jurors. Berman et al. (1995) examined the effectiveness of cross-examination in discrediting inconsistent eyewitness testimony. Participants watched a mock deposition of a bank teller who witnessed a robbery. The video deposition included both direct and cross-examination. In the deposition, the eyewitness responded with either consistent or inconsistent statements regarding central or peripheral details. The inconsistencies that were brought to attention in the cross-examination were between the witness's out-of-court statements and what she said at the deposition. The results revealed that mock jurors who, through cross-examination, were exposed to inconsistency in eyewitness testimony perceived the eyewitness as less credible and the defendant as less culpable; thus, they were less likely to convict the defendant. The authors argued that reduction in guilty verdicts might be mediated by the cross-examination; however, they acknowledged that the effects could be mediated by other factors as well.

Regarding jailhouse informant testimony and cross-examination, there is some promise of attenuating the impact of jailhouse informants based on the above findings concerning inconsistencies in testimony. This promise is based on the archival analysis, noted earlier, of DNA exonerations involving jailhouse informants that indicated that inconsistencies in jailhouse informant testimony occurred about 60 percent of the time (Neuschatz et al., 2020). This included inconsistency between jailhouse informants' testimony and actual case facts, and inconsistency between jailhouse informants' testimony and what they had previously reported to the police or prosecutor. However, it is clear from prior research that impeaching jailhouse informants during cross-examination about any incentive they may be receiving (Neuschatz et al., 2008), their prior record (Neuschatz et al., 2020), or the number of times they testified in the past (Neuschatz et al., 2012) is not effective.

Regarding why cross-examination might impact jurors, research by Wheatcroft and Ellison (2012) showed that the effect of cross-examination may be mediated by witness preparation and the complexity of the cross-examination questions. In this study, community members observed a video of a crime, and then each participant was cross-examined by a practicing lawyer. Participants received either a complex cross-examination or a simpler but equivalent version. The complex cross-examination contained complex vocabulary, leading and multipart questions, and double negatives. By contrast, the simply phrased cross-examination contained less complex vocabulary with no double negatives. In addition, half the participants were allowed preparation on the cross-examination in the form of a guidance booklet about the function of cross-examination; the other half received no familiarization to the process. The authors found that familiarization of witnesses to cross-examination processes increased accurate responses and led to fewer errors about crime details. The authors suggested that advance written information regarding the cross-examination may potentially help to immunize against negative lawyerly influence.

Jury Instructions

Only recently, within the past thirty-five years, have federal and state courts started to recommend that judicial instructions be given about cooperating witnesses like jailhouse informants. For example, the Fifth Circuit Court of Appeals in *US v. Cervantes-Pacheco* (1987) ruled that a trial court should give a special instruction regarding the credibility of witnesses who have been compensated for their testimony. State courts then followed suit; in 1999, the Montana Supreme Court ruled that when a jailhouse informant testifies for personal gain, the court must give a special instruction to the jury. If the trial court fails to give these instructions, and the testimony was crucial to conviction, the conviction must be overturned as a matter of law (*State v. Grimes*, 1999). In 2000, the Oklahoma Criminal Court of Appeals also ruled that courts must give a special instruction when jailhouse informants testify (*Dodd v. State*, 2000). States such as Colorado and Ohio require similar instructions for cases in which there is a jailhouse informant (see Call, 2001). Finally, the Connecticut Supreme Court extended their special jury instruction law (originally only for accomplices) to include jailhouse informants (see *State v. Patterson*, 2005). The Connecticut Supreme Court added jailhouse informants to the law because it was opined that jailhouse informants who have a deal for their testimony have a strong interest to implicate the accused.

The US Supreme Court has emphasized the important and protective nature of jury instructions against unreliable informant testimony in several cases (*Banks v. Dretke*, 2004; *Hoffa v. US*, 1966; *Lee v. US*, 1952). The goal of these instructions is to alert the jurors about the factors they should consider when determining the veracity of jailhouse informant testimony (*State v. Patterson*, 2005). More specifically, the instructions encourage the jurors to consider the motives of the informant and to be cautious when weighing the testimony in their final decision. The instructions contain eight factors (see below for Connecticut Criminal Jury Instructions 2.5–3, 2019). Several states, such as Montana, California, Illinois, and Oklahoma, have implemented similar jailhouse informant jury instructions (The Justice Project, 2007).

> Connecticut Criminal Jury Instructions 2.5–3
> A witness testified in this case as an informant. An informant is someone who is currently incarcerated or is awaiting trial for some crime other than the crime involved in this case and who obtains information from the person on trial regarding the crime in this case and agrees to testify for the state. You must look with particular care at the testimony of an informant and scrutinize it very carefully before you accept it. You should determine the credibility of that witness in the light of any motive for testifying falsely and inculpating the accused.
>
> In considering the testimony of this witness, you may consider such things as:
> - the extent to which the informant's testimony is confirmed by other evidence,
> - the specificity of the testimony,
> - the extent to which the testimony contains details known only by the perpetrator,
> - the extent to which the details of the testimony could be obtained from a source other than the person on trial, the informant's criminal record,

- any benefits received in exchange for the testimony,
- whether the informant previously has provided reliable or unreliable information,
- and the circumstances under which the informant initially provided the information to the police or the prosecutor, including whether the informant was responding to leading questions.

Like all other questions of credibility, this is a question you must decide based on all the evidence presented to you.

Thus far, only one published study has employed judicial instructions to educate jurors about the unreliable nature of jailhouse informants (Wetmore, Neuschatz, Fessinger, et al., 2020). These researchers investigated how judicial instructions about jailhouse informants affected mock jurors' verdicts as well as their perceptions of the jailhouse informant (including how honest, trustworthy, interested in justice, and self-interested the jailhouse informant appeared, and the believed motivation for the jailhouse informant's testimony). Three different forms of judicial instructions were tested. First, there were the Standard Instructions. These made no mention of the informant and simply asked the participants to reach a verdict. These judicial instructions provided a formal definition of reasonable doubt and informed participants to focus on the facts presented and to ignore any personal opinions. Next were Jailhouse Informant Specific Connecticut Instructions, which are presented above. Finally, there were the Enhanced Jailhouse Informant Specific Connecticut Instructions. The enhanced judicial instructions were the same as the Connecticut Instructions, but with specific examples added for each point noted above. The enhanced instructions retained the same key components of the Connecticut Instructions, such as a list of the factors that may influence a jailhouse informant's credibility and the definition of "jailhouse informant." In addition, the enhanced instructions included explanations of how each factor would contribute to the reliability or unreliability of the jailhouse informant. For example, participants were still advised to pay attention to the extent to which the informant's testimony was corroborated by other evidence (as in the Connecticut Instructions), but the enhanced judicial instructions also informed them that jailhouse informant testimony tends to be more reliable when it is confirmed by other evidence and less reliable when it is not. In the study, Wetmore, Neuschatz, Fessinger, et al. also manipulated the reliability of the informant, changing the informant's testimony to align with the instructions if they were reliable. For instance, a reliable witness would not be receiving an incentive for testifying, whereas the unreliable informant indicated that he was receiving a five-year reduction to his sentence.

The results from Wetmore, Neuschatz, Fessinger, et al. (2020) showed that regardless of the instruction type or the reliability of the informant, participants were more likely to convict when a jailhouse informant (51.5 percent) was present compared to a no-jailhouse-informant control condition (23.5 percent). Although participants apparently did not rely on the instructions to help them determine the verdict, they did use the guidelines to evaluate the jailhouse informant. More specifically, when participants were presented with an unreliable jailhouse informant, they rated him as significantly less honest (7.25 vs. 6.21),[3] less trustworthy (7.08 vs. 5.86), less interested in justice (6.57 vs. 5.31), and more self-serving (7.53 vs. 8.91), when compared to the groups who read about the reliable jailhouse informant. This suggests that jailhouse-informant-specific judicial instructions helped educate the jurors in assessing the jailhouse informant's testimony, yet these judicial instructions still failed to translate into better-informed verdicts.

Wetmore, Neuschatz, Fessinger, et al. (2020) was the first study to investigate jailhouse-informant-specific instructions; it would be imprudent to make sweeping generalizations based on only one study. Furthermore, the research has several limitations that make any generalizations premature. The first and most obvious limitation—and this is true of almost all the studies discussed in jailhouse informant research—is that participants rendered individual jury decisions and did not deliberate as they normally would in an actual jury trial. We know from legal decision-making research that deliberation can reduce some juror biases (Bornstein & Greene, 2017; Salerno & Diamond, 2010). Thus, in the case of an unreliable jailhouse informant, jury deliberation might encourage more discussion about the informant and about the cautionary instructions administered by the judge. This discussion could alter jurors' attributions or make these attributions more salient through discussion, thereby moving their evaluation of the jailhouse informant's testimony in a more legally appropriate direction (i.e., better reflecting the strength of the evidence). This is, of course, an empirical question that can be resolved only through further experimentation. It is also entirely possible that discussion could further polarize juries and make individual jurors' opinions more extreme.

The second limitation of the Wetmore, Neuschatz, Fessinger, et al. (2020) study was that participants were presented one set of instructions from one state or an enhanced version of the instructions from that state. As we mentioned earlier, several states have adopted some form of informant-specific instructions. All these state instructions are slightly different and emphasize different aspects of informant testimony. It is possible that although the Connecticut and enhanced Connecticut instructions were ineffective, informant-specific instructions from other jurisdictions may be more effective at combatting unreliable jailhouse informant testimony.

It also may be true that different jailhouse informant instructions, possibly incorporating instructional aids, would have successfully educated mock jurors on the nature of these informants' testimony. Pawlenko et al. (2013) investigated whether instructional aids could improve mock jurors' evaluation of eyewitness evidence. Before reading a trial, participants received one of three aids: a jury duty aid, the *Neil v. Biggers* aid, or an I-I-Eye aid. In the jury duty aid condition, participants were presented traditional instructions that a jury would receive at trial—remain impartial and consider all the evidence before arriving at a decision. In the *Neil v. Biggers* aid condition, participants were given five criteria from this specific case (i.e., eyewitness confidence, the view that the eyewitness had, the time that elapsed between the incident and identification, the attention that the witness paid to the culprit, and the description given by the witness) and were asked to use these criteria when evaluating the eyewitness evidence. In the I-I-Eye condition, participants were instructed to evaluate (a) the eyewitness interview, (b) the identification procedure, and (c) the eyewitness factors at the crime scene (e.g., cross-race vs. same race, weapon focus, head covering, and so forth). Participants, who were college students, received instructions for a particular condition and then read a trial that contained either strong evidence (i.e., the police followed proper procedures for eyewitness testimony) or weak evidence (i.e., the police did not follow proper procedures for eyewitness testimony). The results showed that only participants who were exposed to the I-I-Eye instructional aid demonstrated sensitivity to the eyewitness evidence; they voted guilty more in the strong-evidence case compared to the weak-evidence case.

However, not all studies have found jury instructions in a non-jailhouse-informant trial to be effective. For example, a meta-analysis by Steblay et al. (2006) found a limited effect of jury instructions to disregard inadmissible evidence. In this study, 175 hypothesis tests from 48 studies (8,474 participants) were examined. Steblay et al. found that inadmissible evidence had a consistent effect on verdicts in line with the content of the inadmissible evidence. That is, both defense-slanted and prosecution-slanted inadmissible evidence affected verdicts in favor of the slanted evidence. Furthermore, the authors found that judicial instructions had little to no impact on mitigating the effect of inadmissible evidence. However, when judges provided a rationale for a ruling of inadmissibility, the effect of inadmissible evidence was reduced. Therefore, the evidence on jury instructions suggests that they have a significant but limited effect on jurors' decisions and that the courts may be overly optimistic in their presumption about the safeguarding nature of jury instructions concerning unreliable jailhouse informant evidence.

Additionally, it stands to reason that for jurors to effectively use the judicial instructions, they must first understand the instructions. Without a thorough understanding of judicial instructions, it may be impossible for jurors to comply with and correctly apply the instructions. Unfortunately, the psychological literature suggests that jurors have difficulty understanding judicial instructions (Ogloff & Rose, 2005). For example, Ogloff (1998) examined the comprehension of judicial instructions with more than five hundred jury-eligible participants. In this study, mock jurors watched a two-and-a-half-hour simulated video trial and then deliberated in groups. The videotaped trial included lengthy judicial instructions, like those typically used in real trials. Thus, this experimenter went to great lengths to ensure that the experiment simulated real-life conditions in actual jury trials so the results would be generalizable to actual judicial settings. The results revealed that mock jurors had very little comprehension of the judicial instructions (Ogloff & Rose, 2005).

Ultimately, judicial instructions regarding jailhouse informants may be effective to the extent that they are explanatory and comprehensible. The instructions that were more effective at educating mock jurors were more explanatory, were more comprehensible, and contained less legal jargon (Pawlenko et al., 2013). To the extent that jailhouse-informant-specific judicial instructions conform to these standards, there may be a better chance that these instructions will be effective at sensitizing jurors to the problems with jailhouse informant testimony, without biasing the jurors to totally dismiss the testimony when the jailhouse informant is telling the truth.

Summary

As we have seen, the US Supreme Court has indicated that the trial mechanisms of expert testimony, cross-examination, and judicial instructions are sufficient to protect against unreliable jailhouse informant testimony (*Hoffa v. US*, 1966). Yet careful examination of the literature suggests that these safeguards may have some protective effect but may be confined to a narrow set of circumstances and are therefore not effective for most cases. We should note, however, that researchers like DeLoach et al. (2020) and Wetmore, Neuschatz, Fessinger, et al. (2020) have tested only one safeguard (i.e., informant-specific instructions or cross-examination) in isolation. It may be the case that there are cumulative effects of using several safeguards—expert testimony, cross-examination, and judicial instructions—during trials. Future research should examine whether a combination of these safeguards is more effective in sensitizing jurors to informant reliability.

Conclusion

Recommendations Concerning Jailhouse Informant Testimony

> Because of the perverse and mercurial nature of the devils with whom the criminal justice system has chosen to deal, each contract for testimony is fraught with the real peril that the proffered testimony will not be truthful, but simply factually contrived to "get" a target of sufficient interest to induce concessions from the government. Defendants or suspects with nothing to sell sometimes embark on a methodical journey to manufacture evidence and to create something of value, setting up and betraying friends, relatives, and cellmates alike. Frequently, and because they are aware of the low value of their credibility, criminals will even go so far as to create corroboration for their lies by recruiting others into the plot.
> —Trott (1996)

Throughout this book we have discussed the potential dangers of unreliable jailhouse informants, as echoed in this chapter's epigraph by US Circuit judge Stephen Trott—a longtime critic of the use of cooperating witnesses such as jailhouse informants. We have made two key points throughout the volume. First, jailhouse informants have an enormous motivation to fabricate testimony. Second, when they do testify, they are extremely persuasive. To make these points, we have presented many known cases of false testimony from jailhouse informants, some of whom made a career out of providing false testimony, and we have reviewed the scientific literature related to this testimony. We have also discussed how jailhouse informants, to an extent, may be truthful and can provide an enormous benefit to the criminal justice system and to society. As noted in our discussion of the history of jailhouse informants, they have allowed the government access to information about crimes and criminals they would otherwise not have had. Indeed, proponents of the use of jailhouse informants indicate that they are essential to the criminal justice system and to the administration of justice. Without these jailhouse informants, many crimes might go unsolved (Covey, 2014; Richman, 1996).

We acknowledge that the use of jailhouse informants can benefit the legal system. However, we also emphasize that when relying on criminals or suspects, there is always the possibility that they will flout the law and present false evidence and/or testimony—as has happened throughout the history of the informer system. Given the current legal status of jailhouse informant testimony—it is allowed in most circumstances—and that there is no rush to change existing laws (but see Richman, 1996), we believe it behooves the criminal justice system as well as society to establish a set of minimal necessary guidelines to ensure that jailhouse informant testimony is truthful (see Joy, 2007; The Justice Project, 2007). In this conclusion we outline recommended measures that prosecutors, judges, defense attorneys, and legislators can adopt to prevent (or at the very least reduce) false testimony from jailhouse informants. These recommendations include both novel suggestions and those based on previous proposals raised by others in various disciplines (e.g., law). In either case, the recommendations acknowledge that jailhouse informants have a strong motivation to lie and are designed to ensure that testimony from jailhouse informants is truthful.

As noted by Joy (2007), when false testimony is admitted into a trial, the justice system becomes derailed. This derailment results in an unequal playing field, where the resources and legal expertise of the state are unbalanced with those of the defense (see *Miranda v. Arizona*, 1966). As noted by Goodell (2003), one cannot downplay the importance of equalizing the sides in a trial. By equalizing the sides, the legal system aims to present a context where the truth is more likely to appear and where there is more concern for the moral or normative authority of the judicial system. The recommendations we outline below are designed with these goals in mind.

Prosecutors

A prosecutor's duty is to seek the truth and to uphold justice. To this end, the US Supreme Court in *Berger v. US* (1935) stated that prosecutors should prosecute the guilty and exonerate the innocent. In dispatching this duty, it is a prosecutor who decides what evidence to bring forward at trial. Therefore, it is the prosecutor who decides whether to employ a jailhouse informant. It is also the prosecutor's duty to determine when and what information needs to be turned over, in accordance with the *Brady* rule (*Brady v. Maryland*, 1963), to the defense counsel. Since the decision to use a jailhouse informant is solely that of a prosecutor, we recommend several steps that each prosecutor should take to facilitate valid testimony. For example, prosecutors should

1. require independent corroboration of jailhouse informant testimony
2. record all interactions with jailhouse informants
3. keep detailed records of all cases in which a jailhouse informant has appeared
4. keep detailed records of a jailhouse informant's criminal past
5. disclose all discussions and decisions made regarding benefits that the jailhouse informant is receiving or may receive
6. disclose any benefits the jailhouse informant has received for prior testimony

Approximately seventy years ago, the US Supreme Court recognized that jailhouse informants are prone to present false testimony when the Court indicated that cooperating witnesses raise serious credibility concerns (*Lee v. US*, 1952). According to Joy (2007), the lack of credibility of jailhouse informants should be a paramount concern to the prosecutors who have a duty to the truth. To diminish this concern, Joy argues (and we concur) that prosecutors who make the decision to employ jailhouse informants should require corroboration of their testimony. This recommendation was echoed by the American Bar Association (ABA) Ministry of the Attorney General (1998) report. In their report, the ABA listed the factors regarding jailhouse informants developed by the Kaufman Commission report investigating the wrongful conviction of Guy Paul Morin (Ministry of the Attorney General, 1998).[1] Among the commission's recommendations for dealing with jailhouse informants was to require corroboration of their testimony. More specifically, the Kaufman Commission recommended that any statements from jailhouse informants be corroborated by evidence other than the testimony of other informants. However, it is important to realize that, generally, in the cases in which jailhouse informants testify, there is very little evidence (see Neuschatz et al., 2020).

In addition to requiring corroboration, many commentators (Joy, 2007; The Justice Project, 2007; Natapoff, 2009) have called for prosecutors to keep detailed records of their interactions with jailhouse informants, and we agree with this recommendation. This includes recording each interaction with a jailhouse informant, any deal(s) offered to a jailhouse informant, all past crimes committed by a jailhouse informant, all cases in which a jailhouse informant has testified in the past, and all deals a jailhouse informant has received for prior testimony. One of the simplest methods prosecutors can use to preserve records of working with jailhouse informants as well as fulfill their obligations under *Brady v. Maryland* (1963) is to videotape or audiotape all interactions with a jailhouse informant. These recordings would serve many important purposes.

First, having a full record of all interactions would ensure that any deals or promises made to the informant would be turned over to the defense and preserved for trial. This alone would allow the defense a better chance to effectively cross-examine jailhouse informants when they testify. Second, the recordings should discourage police officers from inadvertently or intentionally providing information about the crime to the jailhouse informant. However, if such information is disclosed, the defense will be able to examine a recording to understand exactly what was disclosed. We should note that research has found that police are significantly impacted by their knowledge of being recorded. For example, Kassin et al. (2014) investigated whether the presence of a recorder would deter interrogators from using psychologically coercive interrogation tactics. The authors had police officers interrogate a suspect who was or was not guilty of committing a staged crime. Some officers were informed that the interrogations would be recorded, while others were not. As expected, police who were informed that they were being recorded were less likely to use psychologically coercive tactics and were perceived by the mock suspect as not trying as hard to get them to confess. In the context of secondary confessions, the results of Kassin et al. (2014) imply that recording police officers would make them less likely to offer information about a case to a jailhouse informant.

The impact of recordings on police interrogations was also shown in another experiment by Kassin et al. (2017). The first phase of this experiment was like the Kassin et al. (2014) study; real police officers investigated a mock crime, interrogated two innocent suspects, and filled out a police report as they would typically do when there was a real crime. Unknown to the police officers, all the interrogations were videotaped. In the second phase lay participants read about the case and then read either the police officers' report or a verbatim transcript of the video. Participants who read a report, relative to those who read a transcript, indicated the process as less pressure filled and were more likely to misjudge suspects as guilty. Thus, police downplayed their use of coercive techniques in their reports—a recording makes clear exactly what happened during an interrogation.

A third benefit of recording all interactions would be to preserve any changes that occur in informants' narratives over repeated interviews. Thus, if jailhouse informants learn new facts and change their story, the prosecution and defense would be aware of these changes. Finally, the audio and/or video recordings can be used by other attorneys who might be dealing with the same jailhouse informants. In this way, these attorneys can be more prepared to impeach jailhouse informants who may have given false testimony in the past.

The proposal of recording all jailhouse informant interactions, as described above, will undoubtedly have its detractors. These opponents may argue that there are practical considerations for not requiring these recordings. For example, recording every jailhouse informant's interaction with the prosecution will lead to significant financial costs and logistical considerations. We should note, however, that resources are always a problem in fighting crime. Of course, one would hope that those politicians who set the budget would be persuaded of the value of recording jailhouse informant interactions. Specifically, fewer false convictions would mean that justice has been served. Moreover, fewer false convictions lead to fewer appeals and fewer trials—a more efficient and cost-effective judiciary. Another concern with recording all interactions with jailhouse informants might be that such recordings will dissuade jailhouse informants from coming forward because they will lose a sense of anonymity from being recorded. In our opinion, jailhouse informants will likely not care about being recorded because they will lose their anonymity once the case goes to trial or is resolved. Their identity will be disclosed to the defendant. Also, even without recordings, every jailhouse informant's identity is known within a jail/prison. Finally, some might argue that recording jailhouse informants will dissuade even honest jailhouse informants from coming forward. However, a study involving primary confessions (Kassin et al., 2019) showed that this may not be the case. In this study, with the help of a city police department, Kassin et al. randomly informed some crime suspects that their interrogations were being video-recorded, while others were not told about the recordings. The results revealed that the suspects who knew that they were being recorded spoke as often and provided as much information as suspects who were not aware of the camera. Thus, in terms of suspects talking about their own crimes, the presence of a camera did not dissuade them from talking to the police.

In dealing with jailhouse informants, some (e.g., Joy, 2007; we concur) have recommended that prosecutors develop specific guidelines for their use. These guidelines should clarify how and when jailhouse informants should be used by both the police (including correctional officers) and prosecutors. For example, the guidelines should indicate the procedures to follow when a jailhouse informant contacts law enforcement. In addition, they should include details about what information offered by a jailhouse informant needs to be gathered, stored, and then turned over to defense counsel before a jailhouse informant can be used in a trial. These guidelines will ensure that all jailhouse informant evidence is handled by the police and prosecutors in a timely and accurate manner. These guidelines should help prevent false testimony in the same way that lineup identification guidelines can help to prevent mistaken identifications. Regarding lineups, in 1999 the US Department of Justice (DOJ) report commissioned by Janet Reno, President Clinton's attorney general (Technical Working Group, 1999), endorsed a set of best practice guidelines for conducting fair and unbiased witness identifications. These guidelines were affirmed and expanded in a memorandum distributed to the heads of all departments of law enforcement entities and all department prosecutors under the Department of Justice (i.e., FBI, Drug Enforcement Administration, Bureau of Alcohol, Tobacco, Firearms and Explosives, US Marshals Service; Yates, 2017).

Judges

Although prosecutors decide what evidence to bring to trial, trial judges serve a critical role during a trial by deciding which evidence is admissible (see Joy, 2007). This gatekeeper role presents judges with the authority to conduct hearings on various types of evidence (including that of expert witnesses) and issue specific instructions. We should note that these trial procedures are typically found in cases involving primary confession. It is our strong recommendation that these procedures be extended for use in *all* cases involving confessions, including secondary confessions, to protect against unreliable jailhouse informants.

Hearings are held to resolve issues without the presence of a jury. Many hearings occur before the trial itself (i.e., pretrial hearings) after motions are raised by attorneys for the prosecution and/or defense. The goal of pretrial hearings is to allow a trial (once the jury is present) to proceed more effectively (LegalMatch, 2020). We should note, however, that during the trial itself, both sides can make motions to the judge regarding the trial. There are many issues that can be raised before a judge (see US Department of Justice, 2020). Note that a judge can rule on a motion at the time it is raised or wait to decide later. Examples of issues raised during pretrial hearings include an attorney (for either side) filing a motion to exclude (i.e., suppress) certain evidence (including that of a witness) because they feel it is tainted in some way (e.g., obtained illegally).

Related to evidence suppression hearings are *Daubert* hearings, which in the context of testifying about jailhouse informants determine whether a proposed expert is qualified to speak about jailhouse informant unreliability, whether the information to be presented at trial by the expert is scientifically sound, and whether the expert's testimony will assist jurors. Given the number of DNA exoneration cases that have involved jailhouse informants, it seems clear that jurors do not fully understand the complexities of jailhouse informant testimony. We believe jurors will benefit from expert testimony in much the same say way they do from primary confession experts and eyewitness experts, both of whom are regularly allowed to testify in court cases. Thus, we recommend that judges allow experts to testify about the unreliability of jailhouse informants.

The need for these psychological experts is exemplified in the case of Arthur Copeland. On April 7, 1998, Andre Jackson was shot to death in Maryville, Tennessee, in an apparent response to the rape of Lynn Porter, the girlfriend of Reginald Stacy Sudderth. The aggrieved boyfriend,

Sudderth, offered a ten-thousand-dollar reward for the murder of the person who raped his girlfriend. During the trial, the prosecution presented evidence that Copeland expressed interest in the bounty and went searching Maryville for the person responsible for the rape. According to an eyewitness, Copeland entered Jackson's house and ordered him outside, at which time Copeland shot and killed Jackson. The defense argued that witness identification was faulty and tried to offer Dr. Jack Brigham as an expert witness on eyewitness identification. The trial court denied the defendant's request to present the expert; Copeland was found guilty and sentenced to death. In 2007, the Supreme Court of Tennessee reversed the Copeland decision on the basis that the trial court erred in not admitting the eyewitness expert (*State of TN v. Copeland*, 2007). The court argued that people do not accurately understand the factors affecting eyewitness identification and that jurors would benefit from the testimony of an expert on these matters. Thus, Copeland was granted a new trial. In 2009, Copeland waived his right to a new trial in favor of a fourteen-year plea agreement for time served. Copeland was released in 2014 (Staff Reports, 2013). Although this example applies to eyewitness experts, we would argue that it also illustrates the need in the courtroom for all social science experts, including experts on jailhouse informants.

Some might argue, given that research on jailhouse informants is relatively new, that an expert on jailhouse informant testimony may not pass the *Daubert* standard testimony criteria (*Daubert v. Merrell Dow Pharmaceuticals*, 1993). However, only considering the relevant research on jailhouse informants grossly underestimates the knowledge of a social scientific jailhouse informant expert. Our view is based on secondary confessions involving a wealth of psychologically related topics: persuasion, social influence, confirmation bias, fundamental attribution error, judgment and decision making, memory, misleading information, deception detection, and self-regulation, as well as many more core principles. Kassin (2007) argued that it is important that experts not undersell themselves and accurately and fully represent the corpus of their expertise and experience. To this end, Kassin presented the pyramid model.

In Kassin's model, the vertex of the pyramid is the information related to the archive of exonerations for the relevant field. In this case, the archival analysis on jailhouse informants (Neuschatz et al., 2020) would be a good resource. Below the vertex is the expert's knowledge of a particular area, which would include psychological experiments, archival analysis, surveys, and field. We have presented this body of research through this book. Finally, at the bottom of the pyramid are the relevant core psychological principles that affect the area in question. For experts on jailhouse informants this would include principles like the fundamental attribution error, confirmation bias, heuristic thinking, deception detection, and so forth. We believe that experts who are introduced more broadly, as opposed to just experts on a specific topic (e.g., secondary confessions), will likely meet the *Daubert* standard as the research on the core principles is voluminous, has been studied over many years, and is generally (if not completely) accepted in the field.

In addition to recommending that expert testimony concerning jailhouse informant reliability be allowed in court, we believe defense attorneys should take full advantage of other legal procedures. For example, defense attorneys should file motions for pretrial hearings requesting that the prosecution release (in a timely manner) information about jailhouse informants (e.g., testimony history) that they feel is being withheld (i.e., motion for discovery) and/or that the prosecution should preserve all evidence until the defense, or an expert, can evaluate the evidence (i.e., motion to preserve evidence). Judges should strongly consider these defense requests to allow for some degree of equity between the prosecution and defense. Moreover, approving these defense requests should allow for better and more detailed cross-examination by the defense (see Joy, 2007).

In closing this section about pretrial hearings, we recommend the use of pretrial reliability hearings. Due to the unreliable nature of jailhouse informants (see Garrett, 2011), some courts have suggested such hearings, while others have already started having them (see Joy, 2007). For example, in *Dodd v. State* (2000), the Oklahoma Criminal Appeals

Court warned that jailhouse informant testimony should be scrutinized when a jailhouse informant is receiving an incentive for their testimony. Similarly, the Nevada Supreme Court ruled that during the penalty phase of capital cases, secondary confessions concerning the defendant may not be heard unless the trial judges have determined that the testimony is reliable and that sufficient evidence exists to corroborate the testimony (*D'Agostino v. State*, 1992).

Regarding reliability hearings, we should note one major reason that defense attorneys request such hearings is that judges have the legal authority to grant such hearings at both the federal and state levels. The Federal Rules of Evidence (Michigan Legal Publishing, 2019) allow a trial judge the authority to grant a pretrial hearing concerning the qualification and credibility of a witness. In addition, the rules allow pretrial admissibility hearings outside of the presence of the jury for all confessions. Finally, the Federal Rules of Evidence allow a trial judge to exclude any evidence that is so biased it outweighs the probative value. Given that jailhouse informants may lack credibility and are generally testifying about confessions, albeit secondary as opposed to primary confessions, it seems that judges should grant reliability hearings for jailhouse informants when defense attorneys ask for them. It should also be the case that judges can exclude a jailhouse informant's testimony if they find it is prejudicial or lacks corroboration.

Finally, judges in certain states are required to present jailhouse-informant-specific instructions to jurors. We believe these instructions assist jurors in thinking about jailhouse informant testimony, and we are hopeful that more states will require judges to present these instructions to jurors in all cases that involve jailhouse informants.

Defense Attorneys

As noted above regarding pretrial hearings, it is critical that defense attorneys take an active role to ensure that unreliable jailhouse informant testimony not invade trials. We should add that defense attorneys can—and we recommend that they should—also request, in cases in which judges do not admit jailhouse informant experts, that the expert be allowed to testify outside the presence of the jury so the court can preserve their testimony for appellate issues. Finally, defense lawyers have conferences and trainings to help other defense attorneys prepare for trials that involve jailhouse informants. We think that this is a good practice, and we recommend that they continue this practice and invite social scientists to speak about the most current findings regarding jailhouse informant testimony and mock jurors' perceptions of this testimony.

Regarding defense attorneys communicating with their peers about jailhouse informant issues, we believe such communication can be extremely helpful and informative. In fact, two attorneys have developed a step-by-step playbook, known as the Rat Manual, for defense attorneys dealing with jailhouse informants (Sevilla & Wefald, 2005). This guide makes many useful suggestions for defense attorneys, such as the following:

- Remind the trial judge early and often when jailhouse informants are to testify that there is a heightened risk of false testimony being leaked into the proceedings.
- Find out as soon as possible if there is a jailhouse informant testifying for the prosecution and research the background of this jailhouse informant. More specifically, it will be critical to determine the jailhouse informant's criminal background and learn any incentives the jailhouse informant is receiving for their testimony (see *Giglio v. US*, 1972).
- Do not allow prosecutors to "put their heads in the sand" and claim they had no knowledge that a jailhouse informant was lying. Prosecutors have a duty to investigate the credibility of their witnesses, including jailhouse informants, and turn over all exculpatory evidence to the defense.
- Do not rely on the prosecution to turn over information about the jailhouse informant. Instead, defense attorneys should do their own investigation of a jailhouse informant, including checking criminal records;

interviewing arresting officers, prison guards, and cellmates; contacting family members; and reviewing jailhouse correspondence (including phone calls made from the jailhouse informant to friends and family).
- Investigate the prosecutor's dealings with a current jailhouse informant and other jailhouse informants the prosecutor has used in the past.
- Make a motion for a pretrial hearing to exclude the testimony of the jailhouse informant.
- Have available information (based on the above investigations) that can be used to impeach jailhouse informants when they testify.
- Retain an expert on jailhouse informant unreliability.
- Request special jury instructions regarding the dangers of jailhouse informant testimony.

Legislators

The recommendations we have already discussed involve judicial reforms. However, lessening the impact of unreliable jailhouse informant testimony will require a concerted push by legislators (at all levels). As noted earlier, some states have already started to enact legislative reforms related to jailhouse informant testimony. In 2019, Connecticut passed laws involving jailhouse informants (S.B. 1098, 2019). The state established the first statewide tracking system for jailhouse informants (see also State of Connecticut, Division of Public Defender, 2019). Each prosecutor's office in the state is required to maintain records of jailhouse informants their office used, the content of the jailhouse informant's testimony, and any incentives that were provided. This information is to be collected and maintained in the Governor's Office of Policy and Management, so that attorneys across Connecticut can check to see if a potential jailhouse informant has testified before. In addition, this legislation requires pretrial hearings for jailhouse informants who testify in cases involving rape and murder. Finally, the Connecticut law requires detailed and prompt—within forty-five days of a defense filing—disclosure of jailhouse informant information. The information that must be turned over to the defense includes the substance of the jailhouse informant's testimony, any incentives offered, prior testimony history, and criminal records.

Connecticut is not alone in its legislative efforts, as other states have also enacted legislation to help prevent false testimony from jailhouse informants. For example, Illinois has been one of the pioneer states on jailhouse informant reform. In 2003, based on the recommendation of then-governor George Ryan's Commission on Capital Punishment, Illinois enacted a law requiring pretrial reliability hearings for jailhouse informants in capital cases (Ryan, 2002). We should note, however, that this law became obsolete when Illinois did away with the death penalty in 2011. Recently, the Illinois Senate passed Senate Bill 1830 (IL S.B. 1830, 2018), which expanded pretrial reliability hearings of jailhouse informants in murder, sexual assault, and arson cases. In addition, prosecutors must now disclose jailhouse informants' criminal records, testimony histories, and incentives the jailhouse informants received in exchange for their testimony. Other states proposing or enacting jailhouse informant reforms include the following:

- Texas (enacted in 2017; H.B. 34, 2017) requires prosecutors to track their jailhouse informants as well as provide comprehensive disclosure information to the defense (see also Lucivero, 2017).
- In 2019, Nebraska drafted legislation to increase transparency for jailhouse informants (Nebraska Revised Statute 29-4704, 2019). The legislation, if passed, would require disclosure of information about jailhouse informants, including criminal history, testimony history, and any incentives a jailhouse informant received in exchange for their testimony. The legislation also would require pretrial reliability hearings for jailhouse informants (see also Morfeld, 2019).
- In 2020, Oklahoma enacted a law that requires prosecutors intending to use jailhouse informants to disclose any incentives that a jailhouse informant received, provide a jailhouse informant's criminal history and testimony history, and create a tracking system of jailhouse informants

(OK SB 1385, 2020). The tracking system stores (in a central database) all information about the jailhouse informant, such as the jailhouse informant's criminal record, the number of times that a jailhouse informant has testified, and incentives that a jailhouse informant has received for testifying (see also Chappell, 2020).

- In 2019, Montana introduced Senate Bill 156, which would have required electronic recording of jailhouse informants' statements, extensive disclosure from the prosecution about each jailhouse informant, jailhouse-informant-specific jury instructions, and pretrial reliability hearings (S.B. 156, 2019). Unfortunately this bill was not passed.

Another legislative approach to dealing with jailhouse informants would be to enact more clearly defined guidelines for judges to follow in cases involving a jailhouse informant. For example, Merritt (2003) has argued for a two-tiered inquiry to detect violations of a defendant's Sixth Amendment right to counsel. In Merritt's plan, the first tier involves a court determining whether a jailhouse informant actively engaged the defendant to reveal incriminating information. As a reminder, the importance of this determination is that if the jailhouse informant actively engaged the defendant, then the jailhouse informant's testimony cannot be admitted as it violates the Sixth Amendment (*Kuhlmann v. Wilson*, 1986). Merritt (2003), however, argued that if the jailhouse informant did not actively seek information, then this should lead to a second tier of inquiry, which would involve a more thorough examination of the government's action in the case. This examination would allow for a determination of whether the government created a situation that made it likely for the defendant to incriminate himself to the jailhouse informant. For example, this second tier would investigate whether the government placed a jailhouse informant in the same cell as an unsuspecting defendant. In Merritt's view, such an act on the part of the government is "just as much an act of deliberate elicitation of information as direct questioning" (2003, p. 1353) and thereby violates a broad interpretation of the Sixth Amendment.

Summary

Systematic problems within the criminal justice system regarding the use of jailhouse informants must be addressed to allow justice to be served for all defendants. Although jailhouse informants may provide truthful testimony, throughout this book we have shown through (a) experiments (Robertson & Winkelman, 2017, Swanner et al., 2010), (b) actual DNA exoneration cases (Neuschatz et al., 2020), and (c) archival analyses (Neuschatz et al., 2020) that jailhouse informants may provide false testimony. Thus, the willingness of jailhouse informants to provide false testimony combined with research showing that individuals will lie and cheat if the payoff is high and the chances of getting caught are low (Kajackaite & Gneezy, 2017) is of concern regarding jailhouse informants. One must also keep in mind that getting out of jail or receiving time off from a jail sentence is a significant payoff (Trott, 1996), and (as noted earlier) it is unlikely for a perjury charge to be brought against a jailhouse informant (see Natapoff, 2009). Clearly, the payoff for a jailhouse informant providing testimony is extremely high.

Jailhouse informant testimony will likely continue in the future, and there will always be cases in which this testimony was presented truthfully and helped to convict guilty defendants. At the same time, it is likely that some jailhouse informants will present false testimony and innocent defendants will be sent to jail. Hopefully, evidence will ultimately be collected that frees these innocent defendants. Moreover, we believe the legal system needs to continue working on effective safeguards that will eliminate the false testimony of jailhouse informants from ever being presented in court.

ACKNOWLEDGMENTS

For me (Jeff), my interest in jailhouse informant research started in 2007 when three events occurred in a very short period of time. First, two of my former students, Deah S. Quinlivan and Jessica Swanner, did a presentation in my Psychology and Law class about the West Memphis Three. In this case, three teenage boys, Damien Echols, Jason Baldwin, and Jessie Miskelley, were convicted of the brutal murder of three young boys. During the documentary, a boy who was in jail with Baldwin says that Baldwin confessed to him over a game of cards. Later on, the probation officer of the snitch says that the snitch cannot be trusted and is a known liar. This was my first exposure to jailhouse informants and why the trials for all my original studies are based on the West Memphis Three trial.

Around this time, I was on the student appeals committee at my university, which is responsible for dealing with student misconduct or academic fraud, such as cheating. In one case, two students were accused of cheating on an exam. The faculty member called one of the accused into his office and said either you tell the other student cheated off you or I am failing you. The student told the faculty member what he wanted to hear.

The final event occurred in my consulting as an eyewitness expert. In this case, someone robbed a postal worker who was on his route. The police canvassed the area, and none of the people living in the area reported seeing anything. A short time later a reward was offered for the capture of the culprit. If memory serves, it was about five thousand dollars. After the reward was offered, two people, who were originally interviewed by police, turned over the name of the defendant to the police. These three events, and at my students' behest, got me thinking about the difference between bartered and non-bartered testimony. Ultimately, this led me to my research program investigating jailhouse informants and to write this book with Jonathan, whose interest in victimization and legal decision making has been ongoing for over thirty years.

Nobody can write a book without the help and support of many people. As such there are many people we need to acknowledge. First, we would like to thank Jennifer Hammer, production staff, and New York University Press. Jennifer has been a treat to work with at every stage. She has been supportive and encouraging throughout the project. Second, we benefited from having many students and colleagues look over early drafts of chapters and help with references. We offer our thanks to Allison Tucker, Hannah Crouse, Stacy Wetmore, Baylee Jenkins, and Alexis Le Grand. Third, we owe a huge debt of gratitude to Ethan Golding, who was kind enough to read and edit every chapter in the book, a thankless and tedious job, which he did with competence, patience, and kindness. Finally, I want to thank Margaret Bull Kovera, whom I affectionately call MBK. MBK was the editor of the first jailhouse informant article I ever published. The original reviews were not encouraging, but she had the foresight to ask for a revision and work with me to turn the paper into a publishable article, thereby initiating a new program of research in the field. I thank her for being an astute and compassionate editor, a loyal friend, and a wonderful unpaid counselor. But most of all I thank her for showing me the value of the review process in science.

Writing a book is extremely time-consuming and demanding. And we could not have done it without the love and support of our families. We would like to express our gratitude to Ginger and Daniel Neuschatz, Roni Giberson, and Dara Golding. Thank you for giving us the support to carry on.

NOTES

1. JAILHOUSE INFORMANTS THROUGHOUT HISTORY

1. As readers will see in chapter 6, courts still issue a cautionary warning when there is a jailhouse informant.
2. Langbein (1983) covers a great deal more than the Crown witness system, but for the purpose of this chapter we confine ourselves to the information related to the Crown witness system and the Corroboration Rule.
3. Jean Valjean in Victor Hugo's novel *Les Misérables* is loosely based on Vidocq.

4. DETECTING DECEPTION

1. A complete list of the documents included in the study is available at www.leaonline.com.
2. For comparison purposes, in the Bond and DePaulo (2006) meta-analysis, the rate of judging false statements as being true was 54 percent, and truths were accurately classified 61 percent of the time.

5. PERCEPTIONS OF JAILHOUSE INFORMANTS IN THE COURTROOM

1. The authors noted that the sample of defense attorneys was quite small ($n = 47$) and was recruited through snowball sampling. Thus, because the lawyers were almost all defense attorneys from the southeastern United States and there were so few of them, the data concerning them need to be interpreted cautiously.

6. EXPERT TESTIMONY, CROSS-EXAMINATION, AND JUDICIAL INSTRUCTIONS

1. A *Daubert* hearing is when the judge decides whether an expert will be allowed to testify at trial (see *Daubert v. Merrell Dow Pharmaceuticals*, 1993).
2. Peer review refers to a process of scientific review where others not associated with the work, who are expert on the topic, evaluate the work. It is typical for the peer review to take into account the validity of the methodology as well as the contribution the work makes to science.
3. These questions assessed the extent to which participants felt the jailhouse informant was trustworthy, honest, interested in justice, and interested in serving their own interests using a scale from 0 (*not at all*) to 10 (*extremely*).

CONCLUSION

1 Guy Paul Morin was wrongly convicted of the rape and murder of his nine-year-old neighbor. One of the reasons for his conviction was the false testimony of two jailhouse informants: Mr. X and Mr. May. Morin was acquitted in his first trial but then found guilty in his second trial. The prosecution was granted a second trial because of a mistake made by the judge in the first trial regarding the instructions that he gave the jury about reasonable doubt. DNA evidence later exonerated Mr. Morin and led to an investigation of the wrongful conviction—the Kaufman Commission report. The true name of Mr. X was banned from publication by the trial judge.

BIBLIOGRAPHY

Akehurst, L., Köhnken, G., Vrij, A., & Bull, R. (1996). Lay persons' and police officers' beliefs regarding deceptive behaviour. *Applied Cognitive Psychology, 10*(6), 461–471.
Ala. Code 1975, § 36-18-30 R.
Allwood, C. M., & Granhag, P. A. (1999). Feelings of confidence and the realism of confidence judgements in everyday life. In P. Juslin & H. Montgomery (Eds.), *Judgment and decision making: Neo-brunswikian and process-tracing approaches* (pp. 123–146). Psychology Press.
Anonymous. (1623). *The life and death of Griffin Flood informer. Whose cunning course, churlish manners, and troublesome information molested a number of plaine during people in this city of London.* http://ezproxy.uky.edu.
Appleby, S. C., Hasel, L. E., & Kassin, S. M. (2013). Police-induced confessions: An empirical analysis of their content and impact. *Psychology, Crime, & Law, 19*(2), 111–128.
Arizona v. Fulminante, 59 USLW 4235 (1991).
Asch, S. E. (1956). Studies of independence and conformity: I. A minority of one against a unanimous majority. *Psychological Monographs: General and Applied, 70*(9), 1–70.
Ashcraft, M. H. (2006). *Cognition* (4th ed.). Pearson.
Ashley, M. (2015). The great detectives: Vidocq. *Strand Magazine, 4*. https://strandmag.com.
Backus, L. (2019). Jailhouse witness bill signed into law. *Connecticut News Junkie*. www.ctnewsjunkie.com.
Banks v. Dretke, 540 US 668 (2004).
Baumeister, R. F., & Vohs, K. D. (2007). Self-regulation, ego depletion, and motivation. *Social and Personality Psychology Compass, 1*, 115–128.
BBC News. (2019, June 12). Central park five: The true story behind *When They See Us*. www.bbc.com.
Berger v. US, 295 US 78 (1935).
Berman, G. L., Narby, D. J., & Cutler, B. L. (1995). Effects of inconsistent eyewitness statements on mock-jurors' evaluations of the eyewitness, perceptions of defendant culpability and verdicts. *Law and Human Behavior, 19*(1), 79–88.
Blandón-Gitlin, I., Sperry, K., & Leo, R. (2011). Jurors believe interrogation tactics are not likely to elicit false confessions: Will expert testimony inform them otherwise? *Psychology, Crime & Law, 17*(3), 239–260.

Bloom, R. M. (2002). *Ratting: The use and abuse of informants in the American justice system.* Praeger.
Bloom, R. M. (2005). A historical overview of informants. Boston College Law.
Bond, C. J., & DePaulo, B. M. (2006). Accuracy of deception judgments. *Personality and Social Psychology Review, 10*(3), 214–234.
Bornstein, B. H., Golding, J. M., Neuschatz, J., Kimbrough, C., Reed, K., Magyarics, C., & Luecht, K. (2017). Mock juror sampling issues in jury simulation research: A meta-analysis. *Law and Human Behavior, 41*(1), 13–28.
Bornstein, B. H., & Greene, E. (2017). *The jury under fire: Myth, controversy, and reform.* Oxford University Press.
Bornstein, B. H., & McCabe, S. G. (2005). Jurors of the absurd? The role of consequentiality in jury simulation research. *Florida State Law Review, 32*(2), 443–468.
Bornstein, B. H., & Neuschatz, J. S. (2020). *Hugo Münsterberg's psychology and law: A historical and contemporary assessment.* Oxford University Press.
Brady v. Maryland, 373 US 83 (1963).
Brewer v. Williams, 430 US 387 (1977).
Bribery of Public Officials and Witnesses, 18 US Code § 201.
Brigham, J. C. (1999). What is forensic psychology, anyway? *Law and Human Behavior, 23*(3), 273–298.
Brown v. Mississippi, 297 US 278, 56 S. Ct. 461 (1936).
Bruggeman, E. L., & Hart, K. J. (1996). Cheating, lying, and moral reasoning by religious and secular high school students. *Journal of Educational Research, 89*(6), 340–344.
Call, J. (2001). Judicial control of jailhouse snitches. *Justice System Journal, 22*(1), 73–83.
CBS News. (2019, June 11). Central Park Five prosecutor Linda Fairstein calls Netflix series an "outright fabrication." www.cbsnews.com.
Chappell, D. (2020, July 15). Oklahoma enacts jailhouse informant law, joins other states. *Criminal Legal News.* www.criminallegalnews.org.
Chojnacki, D. E., Cicchini, M. D., & White, L. T. (2007). An empirical basis for the admission of expert testimony on false confessions. *Arizona State Law Journal, 40*(1), 1–45.
Clare, D. D., & Levine, T. R. (2019). Documenting the truth-default: The low frequency of spontaneous unprompted veracity assessments in deception detection. *Human Communication Research, 45*(3), 286–308.
Colb, S. F. (2008). Hearsay, the Sixth Amendment, and framers' intent: The U.S. Supreme Court hears argument in *Giles v. California.* FindLaw. https://supreme.findlaw.com.
Colloff, P. (2019, December 4). How this con man's wild testimony sent dozens to jail, and 4 to death row. *New York Times Magazine.*
Conliffe, C. (2019, April 12). Eugène François Vidocq, French criminal turned detective. *HeadStuff.* www.headstuff.org.

Connecticut Criminal Jury Instructions, § 2.5-3 (2019).
Cook, L. (2019, June 18). Central Park Five: What to know about the jogger rape case. *AMNY* www.amny.com.
Costanzo, M., Krauss, D., & Pezdek, K. (Eds.). (2007). *Expert psychological testimony for the courts*. Lawrence Erlbaum.
Costanzo, M., Shaked-Schroer, N., & Vinson, K. (2010). Juror beliefs about police interrogations, false confessions, and expert testimony. *Journal of Empirical Legal Studies, 7*(2), 231–247.
Covey, R. D. (2014). Abolishing jailhouse snitch testimony. *Wake Forest Law Review, 49*(5), 1375–1545. https://readingroom.law.gsu.edu.
Coy v. Iowa, 487 US 1012 (1988).
Cutler, B. L., Dexter, H. R., & Penrod, S. D. (1989). Expert testimony and jury decision making: An empirical analysis. *Behavioral Sciences & the Law, 7*(2), 215–225.
Cutler, B. L., Findley, K. A., & Moore, T. E. (2014). Interrogations and false confessions: A psychological perspective. *Canadian Criminal Law Review, 18*, 153–170.
Culter, B. L., & Kovera, M. B. (2011). Expert psychological testimony. *Current Directions in Psychological Sciences, 20*(1), 53–57.
Cutler, B. L., Neuschatz, J. S., & Honts, C. R. (2020, May). An overview of expert psychological testimony in false confession cases. *The Champion*.
D'Agostino v. State, 823 P.2d 283 (Nev. 1992).
Daubert v. Merrell Dow Pharmaceuticals, Inc., 509 US 579, 113 S. Ct. 2786 (1993).
Davies, R. (2017). How successful was the common informer system and how were they perceived in Tudor and Stuart England? Smuggler's City Project, University of Bristol. www.bristol.ac.uk.
Davis, D., & Leo, R. A. (2012). Interrogation-related regulatory decline: Ego depletion, failures of self-regulation, and the decision to confess. *Psychology, Public Policy, and Law, 18*(4), 673–704.
Delaware v. Fensterer, 474 US 15 (1985).
DeLoach, D. K., Neuschatz, J. S., Wetmore, S. A., & Bornstein, B. H. (2020). The role of ulterior motives, inconsistencies, and details in unreliable jailhouse informant testimony. *Psychology, Crime & Law, 26*(7), 667–686.
DePaulo, B. M., Kashy, D., Kirkendol, S., Wyer, M., & Epstein, J. (1996). Lying in everyday life. *Journal of Personality and Social Psychology, 70*(5), 979–995.
DePaulo, B. M., Lindsay, J. J., Malone, B. E., Muhlenbruck, L., Charlton, K., & Cooper, H. (2003). Cues to deception. *Psychological Bulletin, 129*(1), 74–118.
DePaulo, B. M., & Pfeifer, R. L. (1986). On-the-job experience and skill at detecting deception. *Journal of Applied Social Psychology, 16*(3), 249–267.
Devine, D. J. (2012). *Jury decision making: The state of the science*. New York: New York University Press.
Devine, D. J., & Caughlin, D. E. (2014). Do they matter? A meta-analytic investigation of individual characteristics and guilt judgements. *Psychology, Public Police, and Law, 20*(2), 109–134.

Diamond, S. S. (1997). Illuminations and shadows from jury simulations. *Law and Human Behavior*, 21(5), 561–571.

Dodd v. State (10th Cir. R. 36.3., 2000).

Doody v. Shriro, 596 F. 3d 620 (9th Cir. 2010).

Drizin, S. A., & Leo, R. A. (2004). The problem of false confessions in the post-DNA world. *North Carolina Law Review*, 82, 891–1007. https://scholarship.law.unc.edu.

Edwards, D. C. (2013). Admissions online: Statements of a party opponent in the Internet age. *Oklahoma Law Review*, 65, 532–571.

Ekman, P. (1985). *Telling lies: Clues to deceit in the marketplace, politics, and marriage*. Norton.

Ekman, P. (2001). *Telling lies: Clues to deceit in the marketplace, politics, and marriage* (Rev. ed.). Norton.

Ekman, P., O'Sullivan, M., & Frank, M. G. (1999). A few can catch a liar. *Psychological Science*, 10(3), 263–266.

Fessinger, M. B., Bornstein, B. H., Neuschatz, J. S., DeLoach, D. K., Hillgartner, M. A., Wetmore, S. A., & Bradfield-Douglass, A. (2020). Informants v. innocents: Informant testimony and its contribution to wrongful convictions. *Capital University Law Review*, 48(2), 149–187. www.capitallawreview.org.

Findley, K. A. (2012). Tunnel vision. In B. L. Cutler (Ed.), *Conviction of the innocent: Lessons from psychological research* (pp. 303–323). American Psychological Association.

Findley, K. A., & Scott, M. S. (2006). The multiple dimensions of tunnel vision in criminal cases. *Wisconsin Law Review*, 2, 291–397.

Fiske, S. T., & Taylor, S. E. (2008). *Social cognition: From brains to culture*. McGraw-Hill.

Fla. R. Crim. P. 3.220 (2019).

Flowe, H. D., Finklea, K. M., & Ebbesen, E. B. (2009). Limitations of expert psychology testimony on eyewitness identification. In B. L. Cutler (Ed.), *American psychology-law society series. Expert testimony on the psychology of eyewitness identification* (pp. 201–221). Oxford University Press.

Frontline. (1999). The case that changed leniency deals. www.pbs.org.

Frye v. US, 293 F. 1013 (D.C. Cir. 1923).

Garrett, B. L. (2011). *Convicting the innocent: Where criminal prosecutions go wrong*. Harvard University Press.

George, J. F., & Robb, A. (2008). Deception and computer-mediated communication in daily life. *Communication Reports*, 21(2), 92–103.

Giglio v. US, 405 US 150 (1972).

Gilbert, D. T., & Malone, P. S. (1995). The correspondence bias. *Psychological Bulletin*, 117(1), 21–38.

Global Deception Research Team. (2006). A world of lies. *Journal of Cross-Cultural Psychology*, 37, 60–74.

Gneezy, U., Rockenbach, B., & Serra-Garcia, M. (2013). Measuring lying aversion. *Journal of Economic Behavior & Organization, 93*, 293–300.

Goforth, D. (2019, August 23). "Jailhouse snitch" helped send four men to prison, but her false testimony might help get two of them out. *Enid News & Eagle*. www.enidnews.com.

Golding, J. M., Lynch, K. R., & Wasarhaley, N. E. (2016). Impeaching rape victims in criminal court: Does concurrent civil action hurt justice? *Journal of Interpersonal Violence, 31*(19), 3129–3149.

Golding, J. M., Neuschatz, J. S., Bornstein, B. H., Pals, A. M., & Wetmore, S. A. (In press). The perception of a jailhouse informant in a sexual assault case. *Journal of Police and Criminal Psychology*.

Goodell, M. (2003). Government responsibility for the acts of jailhouse informants under the Sixth Amendment. *Michigan Law Review, 101*(7), 2525–2552.

Goodman, G. S., Levine, M., & Melton, G. B. (1992). The best evidence produces the best law. *Law and Human Behavior, 16*(2), 244–251.

Graham, M. H. (1989). *Modern state and federal evidence: A comprehensive reference text*. National Institute for Trial Advocacy.

Granhag, P. A., Andersson, L. O., Strömwall, L. A., & Hartwig, M. (2004). Imprisoned knowledge: Criminals' beliefs about deception. *Legal and Criminological Psychology, 9*(1), 103–119.

Granhag, P. A., & Vrij, A. (2005). Detecting deception. In N. Brewer & K. Williams (Eds.), *Psychology and law: An empirical perspective* (pp. 43–92). Guilford.

Grice, P. (1991). *Studies in the way of words*. Harvard University Press.

Groscup, J., & Tallon, J. (2016). Theoretical models of jury decision-making. In J. D. Lieberman & D. A. Krouss (Eds.), *Jury psychology: Social aspects of trial processes* (pp. 41–65). Routledge.

Gross, S. R., & Jackson, K. (2015, May 13). Snitch watch. National Registry of Exonerations. www.law.umich.edu.

Gross, S. R., Jacoby, K., Matheson, D. J., & Montgomery, N. (2005). Exonerations in the US 1989 through 2003. *Journal of Criminal Law and Criminology, 95*(2), 523–560.

Gudjonsson, G. H. (2003). *The psychology of interrogations and confessions: A handbook*. John Wiley.

Haegerich, T. M., & Bottoms, B. L. (2004, March). *Effect of jurors' stereotypes of juvenile offenders on pre- and post-deliberation case judgments*. Paper presentation, American Psychology-Law Society, Scottsdale, AZ.

Halevy, R., Shalvi, S., & Verschuere, B. (2014). Being honest about dishonesty: Correlating self-reports and actual lying. *Human Communication Research, 40*(1), 54–72.

Hartshorne, H., & May, M. (1928). *Studies in the nature of character. Vol. 1: Studies in deceit*. Macmillan.

Hartwig, M., & Bond, C. F., Jr. (2011). Why do lie-catchers fail? A lens model meta-analysis of human lie judgments. *Psychological Bulletin, 137*(4), 643–659.

Hartwig, M., Granhag, P. A., & Strömwall, L. A. (2007). Guilty and innocent suspects' strategies during police interrogations. *Psychology, Crime & Law*, 13(2), 213–227.

Hartwig, M., Granhag, P. A., Strömwall, L. A., & Andersson, L. O. (2004). Suspicious minds: Criminals' ability to detect deception. *Psychology, Crime & Law*, 10(1), 83–95.

Hasel, L., & Kassin, S. (2009). On the presumption of evidentiary independence: Can confessions corrupt eyewitness identifications? *Psychological Science*, 20(1), 122–126.

H.B. 34., 2017 Reg. Sess. (TX. 2017).

Heath, B. (2012, December 14). Federal prisoners use snitching for personal gain. *USA Today*. www.usatoday.com.

Henkel, L. A., Coffman, K. A. J., & Dailey, E. M. (2008). A survey of people's attitudes and beliefs about false confessions. *Behavioral Sciences and the Law*, 26(5), 555–584.

Herrnstein, R. J. (1997). *The matching law: Papers in psychology and economics* (H. Rachlin & D. I. Laibson, Eds.). Russell Sage Foundation.

Hoffa v. US, 385 US 293 (1966).

Illinois v. Perkins, 496 US 292 (1990).

IL S.B. 1830 (2018).

Inbau, F. E., & Reid, J. E. (1962). *Criminal interrogation and confessions*. Williams & Wilkins.

Inbau, F. E., Reid, J. E., Buckley, J. P., & Jayne, B. C. (2013). *Criminal interrogation and confessions* (5th ed.). Jones & Bartlett.

Innocence Project. (2019, March 6). Informing injustice: The disturbing use of jailhouse informants. Innocence Project. https://innocenceproject.org.

Innocence Project. (2021). The causes of wrongful conviction. www.innocenceproject.org.

Irving, B., & Hilgendorf, L. (1980). *Police interrogation: The psychological approach* (Royal Commission on Criminal Procedure Research Study No. 1). Her Majesty's Stationery Office.

Jenkins, B. D., Le Grand, A. M., Neuschatz, J. S., Golding, J. M., & Wetmore, S. A. (2021). A snitching enterprise: The role of evidence and incentives on providing false secondary confessions. Manuscript, Department of Psychology, University of Kentucky.

Jenkins, B. D., Le Grand, A. M., Neuschatz, J. S., Golding, J. M., Wetmore, S. A., & Price, J. L. (in press). Testing the forensic confirmation bias: How jailhouse informants violate evidentiary independence. *Journal of Police and Criminal Psychology*.

Jones, E. E. (1990). *A series of books in psychology: Interpersonal perception*. Freeman.

Joy, P. A. (2007). Brady and jailhouse informants: Responding to injustice. *Case Western Reserve Law Review*, 57(3), 619–650.

The Justice Project. (2007). Jailhouse snitch testimony: A policy review. Pew Trust. www.pewtrusts.org.

Kajackaite, A., & Gneezy, U. (2017). Incentives and cheating. *Games and Economic Behavior*, 102, 433–444.

Kalven, H., & Zeisel, H. (1966). *The American jury*. Little, Brown.

Kamisar, Y., LaFave, W. R., Israel, J. H., & King, N. J. (2003). *Modern criminal procedure* (10th ed.). West.

Kassin, S. M. (2007). Internalized false confessions. In M. P. Toglia, J. D. Read, D. F. Ross, & R. C. L. Lindsay (Eds.), *The handbook of eyewitness psychology* (Vol. 1, pp. 175–192). Lawrence Erlbaum.

Kassin, S. M. (2015). The social psychology of false confessions. *Social Issues and Policy Review*, 9(1), 25–51.

Kassin, S. M., Appleby, S. C., & Perillo, J. T. (2010). Interviewing suspects: Practice, science, and future directions. *Legal and Criminological Psychology*, 15(1), 39–55.

Kassin, S. M., Bogart, D., & Kerner, J. (2012). Confessions that corrupt: Evidence from the DNA exoneration case files. *Psychological Science*, 23(1), 41–45.

Kassin, S. M., Drizin, S. A., Grisso, T., Gudjonsson, G. H., Leo, R. A., & Redlich, A. D. (2010). Police-induced confessions: Risk factors and recommendations. *Law and Human Behavior*, 34(1), 3–38.

Kassin, S. M., & Gudjonsson, G. H. (2004). The psychology of confessions: A review of the literature and issues. *Psychological Science in the Public Interest*, 5(2), 33–67.

Kassin, S. M., & Kiechel, K. L. (1996). The social psychology of false confessions: Compliance, internalization, and confabulation. *Psychological Science*, 7(3), 125–128.

Kassin, S. M., Kukucka, J., Lawson, V. Z., & DeCarlo, J. (2014). Does video recording alter the behavior of police during interrogation? A mock crime-and-investigation study. *Law and Human Behavior*, 38(1), 73–83.

Kassin, S. M., Kukucka, J., Lawson, V. Z., & DeCarlo, J. (2017). Police reports of mock suspect interrogations: A test of accuracy and perception. *Law and Human Behavior*, 41(3), 230–243.

Kassin, S. M., Meissner, C. A., & Norwick, R. J. (2005). "I'd know a false confession if I saw one": A comparative study of college students and police investigators. *Law and Human Behavior*, 29(2), 211–227.

Kassin, S. M., & Neumann, K. (1997). On the power of confession evidence: An experimental test of the fundamental difference hypothesis. *Law and Human Behavior*, 21(5), 469–484.

Kassin, S. M., Russano, M. B., Amrom, A. D., Hellgren, J., Kukucka, J., & Lawson, V. Z. (2019). Does video recording inhibit crime suspects? Evidence from a fully randomized field experiment. *Law and Human Behavior*, 43(1), 45–55.

Kassin, S. M., & Sukel, H. (1997). Coerced confessions and the jury: An experimental test of the "harmless error" rule. *Law and Human Behavior*, 21(1), 27–46.

Kassin, S. M., Williams, L. N., & Saunders, C. L. (1990). Dirty tricks of cross-examination: The influence of conjectural evidence on the jury. *Law and Human Behavior*, 14(4), 373–384.

Kassin, S. M., & Wrightsman, L. S. (1980). Prior confessions and mock jury verdicts. *Journal of Applied Social Psychology*, 10(2), 133–146.

Kassin, S. M., & Wrightsman, L. S. (1981). Coerced confessions, judicial instruction, and mock juror verdicts. *Journal of Applied Social Psychology*, 11(6), 489–506.

Kassin, S. M., & Wrightsman, L. S. (1985). Confession evidence. In S. M. Kassin & L. S. Wrightsman (Eds.), *The psychology of evidence and trial procedure* (pp. 67–94). Sage.

Key, K. N., Neuschatz, J. S., Bornstein, B. H., Wetmore, S. A., Luecht, K. M., Dellapaolera, K. S., & Quinlivan, D. S. (2018). Beliefs about secondary confession evidence: A survey of laypeople and defense attorneys. *Psychology, Crime & Law, 24*(1), 1–13.

Kuhlmann v. Wilson, 477 US 436 (1986).

Kukucka, J., & Kassin, S. M. (2014). Do confessions taint perceptions of handwriting evidence? An empirical test of the forensic confirmation bias. *Law and Human Behavior, 38*(3), 256–270.

Kyles v. Whitley, 514 US 419 (1995).

Laird, L. (2016, May 1). Secret snitches: California case uncovers long-standing practice of planting jailhouse informants. *ABA Journal.* www.abajournal.com.

Langbein, J. H. (1983). Shaping the eighteenth-century criminal trial: A view from the Ryder sources. *University of Chicago Law Review, 50*(1), 1–136.

Lappen, L. D. (1987). Note, a reconciliation of Henry and Wilson: The intersection of constitutional rights with procedural review, *Duke Law Journal, 36*(5), 945–963.

The Law Dictionary. (2009). What is leading question? https://thelawdictionary.org.

Leach at 263–64, 168 Eng. Rep. at 235.

Lee v. US, 343 US 747, 757 (1952).

LegalMatch. (2020, May 29). What to expect at a pretrial hearing: Pretrial misdemeanor and felony. www.legalmatch.com.

Leippe, M. R. (1995). The case for expert testimony about eyewitness memory. *Psychology, Public Policy, and Law, 1*(4), 909–959.

Leo, R. A. (2008). *Police interrogation and American justice.* Harvard University Press.

Leo, R. A., & Drizen, S. A. (2010). The three errors: Pathways to false confession and wrongful conviction. In G. D. Lassiter & C. A. Meissner (Eds.), *Police interrogations and false confessions: Current research, practice, and policy recommendations* (pp. 9–30). American Psychological Association.

Leo, R. A., & Liu, B. (2009). What do potential jurors know about police interrogation techniques and false confessions? *Behavioral Sciences & the Law, 27*(3), 381–399.

Levine, T. R. (2014). Truth-default theory (TDT): A theory of human deception and deception detection. *Journal of Language and Social Psychology, 33*(4), 378–392.

Levine, T. R., Kim, R. K., & Hamel, L. M. (2010). People lie for a reason: Three experiments documenting the principle of veracity. *Communication Research Reports, 27*(4), 271–285.

Levine, T. R., Park, H. S., & McCornack, S. A. (1999). Accuracy in detecting truths and lies: Documenting the "veracity effect." *Communication Monographs, 66*(2), 125–144.

Levine, T. R., Serota, K. B., Carey, F., & Messer, D. (2013). Teenagers lie a lot: A further investigation into the prevalence of lying. *Communication Research Reports, 30*(3), 211–220.

Levine, T. R., Serota, K. B., Shulman, H., Clare, D. D., Park, H. S., Shaw, A. S., Shim, J. C., & Lee, J. H. (2011). Sender demeanor: Individual differences in sender believability have a powerful impact on deception detection judgments. *Human Communication Research, 37*(3), 377–403.

Lippert, A., Golding, J. M., Lynch, K. R., & Haak, E. (2017). When a corporation rapes: Perceptions of rape in civil court for corporate defendants. *Psychology, Crime & Law, 24*(7), 703–726.

Los Angeles County Grand Jury. (1990). Investigation of the involvement of jailhouse informants in the criminal justice system in Los Angeles County. http://grandjury.co.la.ca.us.

Lucivero, J. (2017, June 15). Texas governor signs landmark comprehensive legislation to prevent wrongful convictions. Innocence Project. https://innocenceproject.org.

Lynch, K. R., Wasarhaley, N. E., Golding, J. M., & Simcic, T. (2013). Who bought the drinks? Juror perceptions of intoxication in a rape trial. *Journal of Interpersonal Violence, 28*(16), 3205–3222.

Maeder, E. M., & Pica, E. (2014). Secondary confessions: The influence (or lack thereof) of incentive size and scientific expert testimony on jurors' perceptions of informant testimony. *Law and Human Behavior, 38*(6), 560–568.

Maeder, E. M., & Yamamoto, S. (2017). Attributions in the courtroom: The influence of race, incentive, and witness type on jurors' perceptions of secondary confessions. *Psychology, Crime & Law, 23*(4), 361–375.

Maine v. Moulton, 474 US 159 (1985).

Mann, S., Vrij, A., & Bull, R. (2004). Detecting true lies: Police officers' ability to detect suspects' lies. *Journal of Applied Psychology, 89*(1), 137–149.

Marr, J. (1971). Andocides' part in the mysteries and Hermae affairs 415 B.C. *Classical Quarterly, 21*(2), 326–338.

Massiah v. US, 377 US 201 (1964).

McCornack, S. A., & Levine, T. R. (1990). When lies are uncovered: Emotional and relational outcomes of discovered deception. *Communication Monographs, 57*(2), 119–138.

McCornack, S. A., & Parks, M. R. (1986). Deception detection and relationship development: The other side of trust. In M. L. McLaughlin (Ed.), *Communication yearbook* (Vol. 9, pp. 377–389). Sage.

McMahon, T. (2019, October 29). The gang that terrorized Georgian London! *London Ghosts*. https://london-ghosts.com.

Melton, G. B., Petrila, J., Poythress, N. G., & Slobogin, C. (2007). *Psychological evaluations for the courts: A handbook for mental health professionals and lawyers* (3rd ed.). Guilford.

Merritt, M. J. (2003). Jailhouse informants and the Sixth Amendment: Is the U.S. Supreme Court adequately protecting an accused's right to counsel? *Boston College Law Review, 44*(4), 1323–1355.

Michigan Legal Publishing. (2019). *Federal rules of evidence* (2019 ed.).

Milgram, S. (1974). *Obedience to authority: An experimental view*. Harper & Row.
Miller, M. K., Maskaly, J., Green, M., & Peoples, C. D. (2011). The effects of deliberations and religious identity on mock jurors' verdicts. *Group Processes & Intergroup Relations, 14*(4), 517–532.
Millstein, S. (2016, September 7). John Mark Karr made this bizarre false confession. *Bustle*. www.bustle.com.
Ministry of the Attorney General. (1998). Report of the Kaufman Commission on proceedings involving Guy Paul Morin. www.attorneygeneral.jus.gov.on.ca.
Minsker, N. (2009). Prosecutorial misconduct in death penalty cases. *California Western Law Review, 45*(2), 373–404.
Miranda v. Arizona, 384 US 436 (1966).
Morfeld, A. (2019, March 7). Regulations considered for use of jailhouse informants. *Unicameral Update*. http://update.legislature.ne.gov.
Moscovici, S., & Zavalloni, M. (1969). The group as a polarizer of attitudes. *Journal of Personality and Social Psychology, 12*(2), 125–135.
Mote, P. M., Neuschatz, J. S., Bornstein, B. H., Wetmore, S. A., & Key, K. N. (2018). Secondary confessions as post-identification feedback: How jailhouse informant testimony can alter eyewitnesses' identification decisions. *Journal of Police and Criminal Psychology, 33*(4), 375–384.
Moxley, R. S. (2015, May 6). Recent proof of prosecutorial misconduct mirrors OCDA's bad old days. *OC Weekly*. www.ocweekly.com.
Munsterberg, H. (1908). *On the witness stand*. Doubleday.
Myers, D. G., & Bishop, G. D. (1970). Discussion effects on racial attitudes. *Science, 169*(2947), 778–779.
Natapoff, A. (2009). *Snitching: Criminal informants and the erosion of American justice*. New York University Press.
Natapoff, A. (2018, July 11). The shadowy world of jailhouse informants: Explained. *The Appeal*. https://theappeal.org.
National Registry of Exonerations. (2017, March 8). Jerry Watkins. www.law.umich.edu.
Nebraska Revised Statute 29-4704 (2019).
Nesterak, E. (2014, October 21). Coerced to confess: The psychology of false confessions. *Behavioral Scientist*. https://behavioralscientist.org.
Neuschatz, J. S., DeLoach, D. K., Hillgartner, M. A., Fessinger, M. B., Wetmore, S. A., Douglass, A. B., Bornstein, B. H., & Le Grand, A. M. (2020). The truth about snitches: An archival analysis of informant testimony. *Psychiatry, Psychology & Law*.
Neuschatz, J. S., Lawson, D. S., Swanner, J. K., Meissner, C. A., & Neuschatz, J. S. (2008). The effects of accomplice witnesses and jailhouse informants on jury decision making. *Law and Human Behavior, 32*(2), 137–149.
Neuschatz, J. S., Wilkinson, M. L., Goodsell, C. A., Wetmore, S. A., Quinlivan, D. S., & Jones, N. J. (2012). Secondary confessions, expert testimony, and unreliable testimony. *Journal of Police and Criminal Psychology, 27*, 179–192.

Nickerson, R. S. (1998). Confirmation bias: A ubiquitous phenomenon in many guises. *Review of General Psychology*, 2(2), 175–220.

Nunez, N., McCrea, S. M., & Culhane, E. E. (2011). Jury decision making research: Are researchers focusing on the mouse and not the elephant in the room? *Behavioral Sciences and the Law*, 29(3), 439–451.

Ofshe, R. J., & Leo, R. A. (1997). The decision to confess falsely: Rational choice and irrational action. *Denver University Law Review*, 74, 979–1122.

Ogloff, J. (1998). Judicial instructions and the jury. A comparison of alternative strategies. Final report. British Columbia Law Foundation.

Ogloff, J. R. P., & Rose, V. G. (2005). The comprehension of judicial instructions. In N. Brewer & K. D. Williams (Eds.), *Psychology and law: An empirical perspective* (pp. 407–444). Guilford.

OK SB 1385 (2020).

Pawlenko, N. B., Safer, M. A., Wise, R. A., & Holfeld, B. (2013). A teaching aid for improving jurors' assessments of eyewitness accuracy. *Applied Cognitive Psychology*, 27(2), 190–197.

PBS. (1999). The case that changed leniency deals. *Frontline*..

Pennington, N., & Hastie, R. (1986). Evidence evaluation in complex decision making. *Journal of Personality and Social Psychology*, 51, 242–258.

Pennington, N., & Hastie, R. (1988). Explanation-based decision making: Effects of memory structure on judgment. *Journal of Experimental Psychology*, 14, 521–533.

Pennington, N., & Hastie, R. (1993). The story model for juror decision making. In R. Hastie (Ed.), *Inside the juror: The psychology of jury decision making* (pp. 192–224). Cambridge University Press.

People v. Gray, No. 78-CF-124 (Ill. Cir. Ct. Sept. 26–Oct. 2, 1978).

People v. Rainge, No. 78-I6-5186 (Ill. Cir. Ct. 1978).

People v. Restivo, Ind. No. 61322 at RHK-014802, RHK-014866 (N.Y. Dis. Ct. 1986).

People v. Thompson, 753 P. 2d 37 (1988).

People v. Wyniemko, No. CR-94-2001FC at WYN-000333 (Mich. Cir. Ct. Nov. 3, 1994).

Possley, M. (2012). Thomas Lee Goldstein. National Registry of Exonerations. www.law.umich.edu.

Possley, M. (2014, August 3). Fresh doubts over a Texas execution. *Washington Post*. www.washingtonpost.com.

Possley, M. (2015, March 9). A dad was executed for deaths of his 3 girls. Now a letter casts more doubt. *Washington Post*. www.washingtonpost.com.

Possley, M. (2021). Alfred Swinton. National Registry of Exonerations. www.law.umich.edu.

Queally, J. (2019, April 21). Five years later, some fear Orange County jail snitch scandal will go unpunished. *Los Angeles Times*. www.latimes.com.

R. v. Atwood and Robbins, 1 Leach 464, 168 E.R. 334 (1788).

Redlich, A. D., Summers, A., & Hoover, S. (2009). Self-reported false confessions and false guilty pleas among offenders with mental illness. *Law and Human Behavior, 34*(1), 79–70.

Reeder, G. D., Vonk, R., Ronk, M. J., Ham, J., & Lawrence, M. (2004). Dispositional attribution: Multiple inferences about motive-related traits. *Journal of Personality and Social Psychology, 86*(4), 530–544.

Reik, T. (1959). *The compulsion to confess: On the psychoanalysis of crime and punishment*. Farrar, Straus & Cudahy.

Rich, M. L. (2010). Coerced informants and Thirteenth Amendment limitations on the police-informant relationship. *Santa Clara Law Review, 50*(3), 681–745.

Richman, D. (1996). Cooperating defendants: The costs and benefits of purchasing information from scoundrels. *Federal Sentencing Reporter, 8*(5), 292–295.

Roberts, S. (2005). Should prosecutors be required to record their pretrial interviews with accomplices and snitches? *Fordham Law Review, 74*(1), 257–302.

Robertson, C., & Winkelman, D. A. (2017). Incentives, lies, and disclosure. *Journal of Constitutional Law, 20*(1), 33–84.

Rohrlich, T. (1988a, October 29). Review of murder cases is ordered: Jail-house informant casts doubt on convictions based on confessions. *Los Angeles Times*. www.latimes.com.

Rohrlich, T (1988b, November 11). A look at jailhouse informants. *Los Angeles Times*. www.latimes.com.

Rohrlich, T. (1989, July 16). Informant switches to the defense: Jail-wise "expert" knows whole truth about lying. *Los Angeles Times*. www.latimes.com.

Ross, L. (1977). The intuitive psychologist and his shortcomings: Distortions in the attribution process. In L. Berkowitz (Ed.), *Advances in experimental social psychology* (Vol. 10, pp. 173–220). Academic Press.

Ross, L., Lepper, M. R., & Hubbard, M. (1975). Perseverance in self-perception and social perception: Biased attributional processes in the debriefing paradigm. *Journal of Personality and Social Psychology, 32*(5), 880–892.

Roth, J. (2016). Informant witnesses and the risk of wrongful convictions. *American Criminal Law Review, 53*(3), 737–797.

Rousseau, B. (2019, September 20). Donald Davidson sentenced to death for 2014 murder of Clay County mom. *Action New JAX*. www.actionnewsjax.com.

Ryan, G. H. (2002). Report of the Governor's Commission on Capital Punishment. https://illinoismurderindictments.law.northwestern.edu.

Saavedra, T. (2017, September 22). Scott Dekraai, Orange County's worst mass killer, gets life without parole for eight Seal Beach murders. *Orange County Register*. www.ocregister.com.

Salaam, Y. (2016, October 12). I'm one of the Central Park Five. Donald Trump won't leave me alone. *Washington Post*. www.washingtonpost.com.

Salerno, J. M., & Diamond, S. S. (2010). The promise of a cognitive perspective on jury deliberation. *Psychonomic Bulletin & Review, 17*(2), 174–179.

Sandys, M., & Dillehay, R. C. (1995). First-ballot votes, predeliberation dispositions, and final verdicts in jury trials. *Law and Human Behavior, 19*(2), 175–195.
S.B. 1098, 2019 Reg. Sess. (CT. 2019).
S.B. 156, 2019 Reg. Sess. (MT. 2019).
Schindler, A. (2019, September 20). "Sometimes the devil creeps in": Donald Davidson's confession tape is an unvarnished look at a brutal crime. *First Coast News.* www.firstcoastnews.com.
Schuller, R. A., & Hastings, P. A. (1996). Trials of battered women who kill: The impact of alternative forms of expert evidence. *Law and Human Behavior, 20*(2), 167–187.
Schuller, R. A., & Stewart, A. (2000). Police responses to sexual assault complaints: The role of perpetrator/complainant intoxication. *Law and Human Behavior, 24*(5), 535–551.
Schwartz, J. (2014, February 28). Evidence of concealed jailhouse deal raises questions about a Texas execution. *New York Times.* www.nytimes.com.
Schweitzer, N. J., & Saks, M. J. (2009). The gatekeeper effect: The impact of judges' admissibility decisions on the persuasiveness of expert testimony. *Psychology, Public Policy, and Law, 15*(1), 1–18.
Serota, K. B., Levine, T. R., & Boster, F. J. (2010). The prevalence of lying in America: Three studies of self-reported lies. *Human Communication Research, 36*(1), 2–25.
Serota, K. B., Levine, T. R., & Burns, A. (2012). *A few prolific liars: Variation in the prevalence of lying.* Paper presentation, National Communication Association, Orlando, FL.
Sevier, J. (2015). Popularizing hearsay. *Georgetown Law Journal, 104*(3), 643–692.
Sevilla, C. M., & Wefald, V. (2005). *The rat manual.* www.charlessevilla.com.
Shaw, J. I., & Skolnick, P. (1995). Effects of prohibitive and informative judicial instructions on jury decision making. *Social Behavior and Personality, 23*(4), 319–325.
Simons, M. A. (2003). Retribution for rats: Cooperation, punishment, and atonement. *Vanderbilt Law Review, 56*(1), 1–56.
Smith, J. (2013). *Criminal evidence: Hearsay.* University of North Carolina, School of Government, Administration of Justice Bulletin. www.sog.unc.edu.
Spanos, N. P., Gwynn, M. I., & Terrade, K. (1989). Effects on mock jurors of experts favorable and unfavorable toward hypnotically elicited eyewitness testimony. *Journal of Applied Psychology, 74*(6), 922–926.
Staff Reports. (2013, September 6). Former death row inmate Copeland charged with Knoxville rape. *Daily Times.* www.thedailytimes.com.
State of Connecticut, Division of Public Defender. (2019). Testimony of Christine Perra Rapillo, Chief Public Defender. https://portal.ct.gov.
State of TN v. Copeland, No. E2002-01123-SC-DDT-DD (2007).
State v. Grimes, 986 P2d 1290 (Or. Ct. App. 1999).
State v. Hernandez, Nos. 84-CF-361-01-12, 84-CF-362-01-12, 84-CF-363-01-12 at HERN-008418, HERN-008419 (Ill. Cir. Ct. Feb. 20, 1985).
State v. Leniart, 149 A.3d 499 (2020).

State v. Patterson, 276 Conn. 452 (2005).

Steblay, N., Hosch, H. M., Culhane, S. E., & McWethy, A. (2006). The impact on juror verdicts of judicial instruction to disregard inadmissible evidence: A meta-analysis. *Law and Human Behavior, 30*(4), 469–492.

Story, K. (2019, June 1). "When They See Us" shows the disturbing truth about how false confessions happen. *Esquire.* www.esquire.com.

Strömwall, L. A., & Granhag, P. A. (2003). How to detect deception? Arresting the beliefs of police officers, prosecutors and judges. *Psychology, Crime & Law, 9*(1), 19–36.

Strömwall, L. A., Granhag, P. A., & Hartwig, M. (2004). Practitioners' beliefs about deception. In P. Granhag & L. Strömwall (Eds.), *The detection of deception in forensic contexts* (pp. 229–250). Cambridge University Press.

Swanner, J. K., Beike, D. R., & Cole, A. T. (2010). Snitching, lies, and computer crashes: An experimental investigation of secondary confessions. *Law and Human Behavior, 34*(1), 53–65.

Technical Working Group for Eyewitness Evidence. (1999). *Eyewitness evidence: A guide for law enforcement.* US Department of Justice, Office of Justice Programs.

Toinkovicz, J. J. (1988). An adversary system defense of the right to counsel against informants: Truth, fair play, and the Massiah Doctrine. *University of California, Davis Law Review, 22,* 1–92.

Trott, S. (1996). Words of warning for prosecutors using criminals as witnesses. *Hastings Law Journal, 47,* 1381–1394.

US Bureau of Justice Statistics. (1984). *United States historical corrections statistics 1850–1984.* www.bjs.gov.

US Bureau of Justice Statistics. (2020). *Prisoners in 2019.* www.bjs.gov.

US Department of Justice. (2020). *Pre-trial motions.* www.justice.gov.

US Sentencing Commission. (1996). *1996 sourcebook of federal sentencing statistics.* www.ussc.gov.

US Sentencing Commission. (2011). *2011 report to the Congress: Mandatory minimum penalties in the federal criminal justice system.* www.ussc.gov.

US Sentencing Commission. (2017). *2017 sourcebook of federal sentencing statistics.* www.ussc.gov.

US v. Cervantes-Pacheco, 826 F.2d 310, 315 (5th Cir. 1987).

US v. Ford, 99 US 594 (1878).

US v. Henry, 447 US 264 (1980).

US v. Khalil, 132 F.3d 897, 898, 3d Cir. (1997).

US v. Singleton, 144 F.3d 1343 (1998).

US v. Singleton, 165 F.3d 1297 (1999).

US v. White, 401 US 745 (1971).

Virginia Criminal Sentencing Commission. (2018). *Virginia criminal sentencing commission annual report 2018.* www.vcsc.virginia.gov.

Vrij, A. (2000). *Detecting lies and deceit: The psychology of lying and implications for professional Practice.* John Wiley.

Vrij, A. (2008). *Detecting lies and deceit: Pitfalls and opportunities* (2nd ed.). John Wiley.

Vrij, A., Granhag, P. A., & Mann, S. (2011). Outsmarting the liars: Toward a cognitive lie detection approach. *Current Directions in Psychological Science, 20*(1), 28–32.

Vrij, A., Granhag, P. A., & Porter, S. (2010). Pitfalls and opportunities in nonverbal and verbal lie detection. *Psychological Science in the Public Interest, 11*(3), 89–121.

Vrij, A., & Mann, S. (2001). Who killed my relative? Police officers' ability to detect real-life high stakes lies. *Psychology, Crime and Law, 1*(2), 119–132.

Vrij, A., & Semin, G. R. (1996). Lie experts' beliefs about nonverbal indicators of deception. *Journal of Nonverbal Behavior, 20*, 65–80.

Vrij, A., Taylor, P., & Picornell, I. (2015). Verbal lie detection. In G. Oxburgh, T. Myklebust, T. Grant, & R. Milne (Eds.), *Communication in investigative and legal contexts: Integrated approached from forensic psychology, linguistics and law enforcement* (pp. 259–286). Wiley-Blackwell.

Wallace, D. B., & Kassin, S. M. (2012). Harmless error analysis: How do judges respond to confession errors? *Law and Human Behavior, 36*(2), 151–157.

Warden, R. (2004). *The snitch system: How incentivized witnesses put 38 innocent Americans on death row.* Northwestern University School of Law, Center on Wrongful Convictions.

Wason, P. C. (1966). Reasoning. In B. M. Foss (Ed.), *New horizons in psychology* (pp. 135–151). Penguin.

Weiten, W., & Diamond, S. S. (1979). A critical review of the jury simulation paradigm: The case of defendant characteristics. *Law and Human Behavior, 3*(1–2), 71–93.

Wenger, A. A., & Bornstein, B. H. (2006). The effects of victim's substance use and relationship closeness on mock jurors' judgments in an acquaintance rape case. *Sex Roles, 54*(7), 547–555.

Wetmore, S. A., Neuschatz, J. S., Fessinger, M. B., Bornstein, B. H., & Golding, J. M. (2020). Do judicial instructions aid in distinguishing between reliable and unreliable jailhouse informants? *Criminal Justice and Behavior, 47*(5), 582–600.

Wetmore, S. A., Neuschatz, J. S., & Gronlund, S. D. (2014). On the power of secondary confession evidence. *Psychology, Crime & Law, 20*(4), 339–357.

Wetmore, S. A., Neuschatz, J. S., Roth, J., Jenkins, B. D., & Le Grand, A. M. (2020). Incentivized to lie: Informant witnesses. In B. Bornstein & M. K. Miller (Eds.), *Advances in psychology and law* (pp. 23–49). Springer.

Wheatcroft, J. M., & Ellison, L. (2012). Evidence in court: Witness preparation and cross-examination style effects on adult witness accuracy. *Behavioral Sciences & the Law, 30*(6), 821–840.

Wheatcroft, J. M., Wagstaff, G. F., & Kebbell, M. R. (2004). The influence of courtroom questioning style on actual and perceived eyewitness confidence and accuracy. *Legal and Criminological Psychology, 9*(1), 83–101.

Wheeler, S., Mann, K., & Sarat, S. (1988). *Sitting in judgment: The sentencing of white-collar criminals.* Yale University Press.

Wiener, R. L., Kraus, D. A., & Lieberman, J. D. (2011). Mock jury research: Where do we go from here? *Behavioral Sciences and the Law, 29*(3), 467–479.

Wigmore, J. H. (1904). *A treatise on the Anglo-American system of evidence in trials at common law*. Little, Brown.

Wigmore, J. H. (1908). A general survey of the history of the rules of evidence. In *Select essays in Anglo-American legal history* (pp. 396–401). Little, Brown.

Wigmore, J. H. (1970). *Evidence* (Vol. 3; revised by J. H. Chadbourn). Little, Brown.

Woody, W. D., Stewart, J. M., Forrest, K. D., Camacho, L. J., Woestehoff, S. A., Provenza, K. R., Walker, A. T., & Powner, S. J. (2018). Effects of false-evidence ploys and expert testimony on jurors, juries, and judges. *Cogent Psychology, 5*(1).

Yates, S. Q. (2017, January 6). *Memorandum for heads of department law enforcement components: All department prosecutors*. US Department of Justice. www.justice.gov.

Yesko, P. (2019, December 16). Curtis Flowers released on bail. *APM Reports*. www.apmreports.org.

Zimmerman, C. (1994). Toward a new vision of informants: A history of abuses and suggestions for reform. *Hastings Constitutional Law Quarterly, 22*(81), 81–178.

INDEX

ABA. *See* American Bar Association
Accomplice Rule, 27
Ackeret, Dennis, 56
admissibility, of testimony, 5–6, 39–40, 145
Alcibiades, 19
Allain, P. J., 123–24
American Bar Association (ABA), 152
Andocides, 18–19
Appleby, S. C., 69
approver informants, 19–21, 23
Arizona v. Fulminante, 6, 42, 73
attribution error, 69

behavioral model, 86
behavior cues, 90
belief preservation, 117
Berman, G. L., 138
Black Boy Alley, 25
Blandón-Gitlin, I., 134
Bloom, R. M., 18
Boblit, Charles, 52–53
body movement, 89–90, 93
Boggio, Shelly, 98–99
Bond, C. J., 84, 91, 167n2 (chap. 4)
Boorn, Jesse, 29–30
Boorn, Stephen, 29–30
Brady, John, 52–53
Brady v. Maryland, 52–54, 124, 151–52
Brewer v. Williams, 43–44
bribery, 34, 40, 49–50
Brigham, Jack, 157
Brown v. Mississippi, 58
Bruggeman, E. L., 105–6

Cane, Charles, 25–26
cautionary instructions, 15
Center for Wrongful Convictions, 7
Central Park Five, 65–66
Charles, Ray, 77
Charles I (king), 22
CID. *See* Criminal Investigation Department
civil rights, 33
Clare, D. D., 84–85
closing statements, 13
coerced confessions, 42, 73
cognitive-behavioral viewpoint, 61
Cole, 26–27
college sample, 82–83
college students, 92–94
Colloff, P., 98
Colson, Gary, 46
Colvin, Russell, 29–30
common informers, 19–21
community members, 72
confessions, 92–94; coerced, 42, 73; conviction rates from, 73–74; high- and low-pressure, 74; involuntary, 73; mock trial methodology for, 70–73; pretrial, 28; psychology of, 57; reasons for, 61; recanting of, 66; theories of, 60–64; totality of circumstances in, 70; United States rates of, 58. *See also* false confessions; primary confessions; secondary confessions
confidential informant, 77
confirmation bias, 117–19
confrontation clause, 136

185

Connecticut Criminal Jury Instructions, 141–42
consensual sex, 3
control group, 73, 105
conversation, lies during, 80
convicted felons, 8, 19–20
convictions: confession rates of, 73–74; cross-examination reducing, 138; expert testimony and, 134; false testimony with, 2, 5, 76–77, 126–27, 167n1 (conclusion); from informant testimony, 143; informant testimony with wrongful, 123–24, 131; secondary confession with wrongful, 129–30. *See also* false convictions
cooperating witness, 17
Cope, Billy Wayne, 65
Copeland, Arthur, 156–57
corroboration rule, 17, 26–27, 36
cost-benefit analysis, 107
counsel, right to, 43, 45–48
Court of Appeals, 104
courtrooms, 157; false confessions in, 69; informant testimony in, 30–35; jury instructions in, 140–46; testimony accuracy in, 119; undisclosed information problem in, 11–12
credibility, 16; of approver informants, 20; of informant testimony, 151–52; prosecution checking, 32–33; ratings, 72–73; of witnesses, 140
crime-fighting tool, 6, 23
criminal investigation, 56
Criminal Investigation Department (CID), 29
criminal justice system, 4, 6, 14, 30–31, 149
criminals, 31, 90, 93–96
criminal trials: defense attorneys preparing for, 160; Federal Rules of Evidence in, 38; informant networks and, 24–25; informant testimony in, 3–4; murder trial and, 125–26

cross-examination, 5, 103; conviction rates reduced by, 138; of informant testimony, 68–69, 118, 124–25, 136–40, 152–53; leading questions during, 137; by prosecution, 39–40; witness preparation of, 139–40
the Crown, 21–23
Crown witness system, 23–28

Dailey, Clarence James, 98–99
Daubert hearing, 167n1 (chap. 6)
Daubert v. Merrell Dow Pharmaceuticals, 6, 125–30, 157
Davidson, Donald, 56
Davies, R., 21
Davis, D., 61
death penalty, 7, 77
deception, 87–89, 95
deception detection: attribution error in, 69; challenges in, 94–96; common predictors of, 89–90; criminals used in study of, 90, 93–94; deception practiced and, 95; difficulty in, 14; of false testimony, 12; jurors have trouble with, 69, 78–79; lie base rate and, 79; low state of suspicion in, 84; for lying, 16; meta-analysis of, 84; methodologies implemented for, 88–89; physical arousal in, 88; by police officers, 16; prosecutors and, 87–88; subjective behavior cues in, 90
deceptive-motive condition, 104–5
decision-making process, 61
defendants, 3–4, 44, 48, 59–60
defense attorneys, 54–55, 158–61, 167n1 (chap.6)
Dekraai, Scott, 33
Delaware v. Fensterer, 136
deliberate-elicitation standard, 48
DeLoach, D. K., 137–38, 147
DePaulo, B. M., 80–81, 84, 93, 167n2 (chap. 4)

dispositional attributions, 69, 114–15
dispositional factors, 110
dispositional motive, 10, 63
district attorney, 31–33, 77–78
DNA evidence: false convictions overturned by, 8–9, 67; false testimony exonerations from, 127–28, 139, 156, 164; informant testimony and, 34–35, 139; Innocence Project and exoneration by, 13; Restivo exonerated by, 37; secondary confessions and, 56
Dodd v. State, 140, 158
Dorfman, Stephen, 37
double standard model, 86, 88
Douglas, Napoleon, 50
due process, 53–54

ecological validity, 71
Edwards, D. C., 39
Elizabeth II (queen), 22
Ellison, L., 139
English judicial system, 24
Enhanced Jailhouse Informant Specific Connecticut Instructions, 142
evidence: eyewitness identification contaminating, 92, 112; fabrication of, 110; forensic, 1–2, 113; inadmissible, 145; from informant testimony, 54–55; jurors influenced by, 111–12, 120; physical or forensic, 1–2, 113; rules of, 55; scientific, 125–26, 131; strong-evidence case as, 145; suppression hearings for, 156; survey research rating types of, 100–102; trial judges hearing, 155–56; types of, 110–11. *See also* DNA evidence
excited utterance, 38
exclusionary rules, 28
exculpatory information, 53–54
expert psychological testimony, 125–35
expert testimony, 124–25; conviction rates and, 134; error rates of, 128–29; false evidence ploys and, 133–34; guilty verdicts from, 131; informant testimony impacting, 124–25, 130–33; research of, 133–35; social scientists offering, 135
explicit judgments, 72–73
extortion, 20–21
eye contact, 89–91, 93
eyewitness: identification, 92, 112; inconsistent testimony of, 139; in police investigation, 1; trial court erred about, 157

FAE. *See* fundamental attribution error
false confessions, 13, 57, 92; in courtroom, 69; interrogation techniques with, 65; secondary, 31
false convictions, 37, 154; DNA evidence overturning, 8–9, 67; factors in, 6–7; jurors persuaded in, 7, 77–79; primary confessions leading to, 65
false evidence ploy, 133–34
false statements, 90, 92, 167n2 (chap. 4)
false testimony, 55; conditions for, 132; conviction overturned and, 2, 5, 76–77, 126–27, 167n1 (conclusion); Corroboration Rule for, 27; in criminal justice system, 14, 30–31; deception detection of, 12; DNA exonerations of, 127–28, 139, 156, 164; guidelines preventing, 155; incentives causing, 64, 108–10; informant testimony and, 149–50, 162; legislation preventing, 162; secondary confessions leading to, 66–67; wrongful convictions from, 126–27
falsification principle, 119
Federal Bribery Statue, 50
federal court decision, 49–50
federal prison system, 99–100
Federal Rules of Evidence, 37–40, 126, 159
feedback, 112, 117
Fessinger, M. B., 143–44, 147
field-based research, 88–92

Fielding, Henry, 27
Fifth Amendment, 41–42
Fink, Edward (Eddie), 1–3, 82, 100
Fleischli, Ginger, 2–3
Flood, Griffin, 21–22
Florida, 35
Flowers, Curtis, 76–78
forensic evidence, 1–2, 113
Fourteenth Amendment, 58
Fourth Amendment, 40–41
Frye Rule, 125, 136
Frye v. US, 125
Fulminante, Oreste, 42
fundamental attribution error (FAE), 10, 110, 114–15, 121, 130

Garrett, B. L., 6
George, J. F., 81
Giglio, John, 53
Giglio v. US, 6, 53
Global Deception Research Team, 90–91
Gneezy, U., 106–7
Goethals, Thomas, 33
Golden (assistant US attorney), 53
Golding, J. M., 111
Goldstein, Thomas, 1–2
Goodell, M., 46, 150
Granhag, P. A., 90
Greece, 17–18
Grice, P., 80
Groscup, J., 120
Gross, S. R., 126
Gudjonsson, G. H., 58, 60
guidelines: for defense attorneys, 160–61; false testimony prevented by, 155; for informant testimony, 150–51; for judges, 163; sentencing, 51–52
guilt/shame, 62
guilty verdicts, 15, 121, 131–32

habitual lying, 83
Halevy, R., 83

Hallmon, Odell, 76–78, 82, 97
handwriting samples, 113
Hart, K. J., 105–6
Hartwig, M., 91, 93
Hastie, R., 120
Hawkins, Maurice, 76–77
hearsay testimony, 38–39
Henry, Billy Gale, 44
heuristic model, 86
high-pressure confessions, 74
high school students, 105–6
high-stakes lies, 94
Hoffa, Jimmy, 40–41
Hoffa v. US, 5, 41, 99, 124, 146
hypothesis tests, 145

I-I-Eye condition, 144–45
illegal search and seizure, 40–41
Illinois v. Perkins, 41–42
implicit prosecutorial vouching, 97, 117–19, 122
incarcerated defendant, 44
incentives: disclosure of, 103, 124–25, 162–63; false testimony caused by, 64, 108–10; federal court decision on, 49–50; for informant testimony, 4–5, 32–33, 45, 49–52, 78–79, 103–4; lies motivated by, 106, 121; perjury for, 107–8; prosecution to disclose, 124–25; safeguards of witnesses receiving, 136; in secondary confessions, 63–64; testimony return for, 8
informant networks: ancient, 18–19; crime deterred by, 23; criminal trials and, 24–25; Middle ages, 19–21; of police officers, 18; Ryder Years, 23–28; in United States, 29–30
informant testimony, 14, 167n3; accurate information from, 68; case overturned due to, 123–24; cautionary instructions concerning, 15; characteristics of, 7–9; of convicted criminals, 8; convictions

from, 143; corroboration issue of, 26–27; cost-benefit analysis of, 107; courtroom testimony in, 30–35; credibility of, 151–52; in criminal trials, 3–4; critical information through, 63; cross-examination of, 68–69, 118, 124–25, 136–40, 152–53; deals brokered with, 101; defendant information in, 3–4, 59–60; defendant targeted with, 48; defense counsel and reliability of, 159–60; DNA evidence and, 34–35, 139; evidence from, 54–55; expert testimony impact on, 124–25, 130–33; false testimony of, 149–50, 162; Federal Rules of Evidence of, 37–40; Florida's rules for, 35; guidelines for, 150–51; guilty verdicts from, 15, 121; history of, 17–18; implicit prosecutorial vouching of, 97, 122; incentives for, 4–5, 32–33, 45, 49–52, 78–79, 103–4; issues in, 7; jurors and, 96–97, 100–101; jurors unaware of dangers of, 134–35; jury instructions on unreliable, 141–43; legal decision making impacted by, 102–14; lie base rate of, 128–29; lying in, 82; mock juror's perceptions of, 121, 144–45; modern day, 29–30; Neuschatz and, 11–13, 60, 67–68; persuasive quality of, 100, 114–21; police officers assisting, 32; pretrial hearing reliability of, 158–59; for prosecution, 2–3, 10, 12–13; psychological research on, 16; psychology of, 4; published study of, 142–46; Rat Manual and, 160; recording of, 154, 163; regulations on, 55; rehearsed responses in, 95; safeguards for, 5–6, 16; as secondary confessions, 5; story model, 120–21; Supreme Court protecting, 6; testimony corroboration with, 152, 159; transparency of, 162; tunnel vision and, 116–19; undisclosed information of, 11–12; unregulated, 100; unreliable, 146–47, 161; wrongful convictions from, 123–24, 131

informant witnesses, types of, 114
information, 11–12, 53–54; accuracy of, 59; coercion of, 66; informant testimony with accurate, 68; informant testimony with critical, 63; informant testimony with defendant, 3–4, 59–60; obtained without counsel, 42–43; technology obtaining, 41
informer system, 18
Innocence Project, 6–8, 13
internalization, 65
interrogation-related regulation decline (IRRD), 61–62
interrogations, 65; police, 1, 58, 91–92; video recordings of, 91–92, 154–55
involuntary confession, 73
IRRD. See interrogation-related regulation decline

Jackson, Andre, 156
Jackson, Harvey, 41
jailhouse informant specific Connecticut instructions, 142
jailhouse-informant-specific instructions, 143–46
Jenkins, B. D., 64, 113
Joy, P. A., 150–51
judges, 27–28, 155–59, 163
jurors: bias reduction of, 144; deception detection of, 69, 78–79; evidence influence on, 111–12, 120; false convictions persuasion and, 7, 77–79; informant testimony and, 96–97, 100–101; informant testimony dangers and, 134–35; informant testimony safeguards for, 5–6, 16; judges cautioning, 27–28; judicial instructions to, 146; pro-prosecution bias of, 119; secondary confessions influencing, 102; witnesses believed by, 116; witness vetting assumed by, 12, 14, 96–97
jury instructions, 140–46

Kajackaite, A., 106–7
Karr, John Mark, 65
Kassin, S. M., 13, 60, 73–74, 153–54; confession rates from, 58; confession videotapes by, 92–93; false primary confessions from, 65; secondary confessions and, 157–58
Kaufman Commission report, 152
Kuhlmann v. Wilson, 47–49, 163
Kyles, Curtis Lee, 54
Kyles v. Whitley, 54

lab-based research, 89, 92–94
laboratory research, 71
Langbein, J. H., 23–24, 26, 28
leading questions, 137
Lee, Benny, 47
legal decision making, 70–71, 102–14
legislation, 161–63
Leippe, M. R., 135
Leitch, David, 2–3
Leniart, George, 123–24
Leo, R. A., 61
Levine, T. R., 79–80, 83–85, 104–5, 116
lie base rate, 79–87, 128–29
lies: body movement and, 89–90; cost-benefit analysis of, 107; deception detection for, 16; distribution of, 81–82; habitual, 83; high-stakes, 94; incentives motivating, 106, 121; by informant testimony, 82; physiological cues to, 88; preparing, 95; in social interactions, 80–81; social-psychological research of, 109; with truthful responses, 95–96; truth-lie judgment and, 85; verbal and nonverbal cues in, 96. *See also* deception
Los Angeles County Grand Jury, 7–11, 31–35, 109
low-pressure confessions, 74

Maeder, E. M., 131
Maine v. Moulton, 45–46

Mann, S., 89, 91, 94
Manufacturers Hanover Trust Company, 53
Massiah v. US, 6, 43, 45
McCornack, S. A., 84, 86
McGinest, John, 1
Mechanical Turk, 72
Meili, Trisha, 65–66
Merill, Silas, 29–30
Merritt, M. J., 163
meta-analysis, 84, 91, 145
Miranda Rights, 113
Miranda warning, 42, 58–59
mock jurors: from guilty verdicts, 131–32; informant testimony perceptions of, 121, 144–45; simulated video trial for, 146, 152; social science arguments and, 135
mock trial methodology, 70–73, 103–5
modern day informants, 29–30
Montana, 163
Morin, Guy Paul, 167n1 (conclusion)
Mote, P. M., 112
Moulton, Perley, 46
Munsterberg, H., 58
murder trial, 125–26

Natapoff, Alexandra, 6–7, 15, 63
national sample, 82–83
Nebraska, 162
negative constraint, 73
Neil v. Biggers, 144
nervousness, 90
Nesterak, E., 66
Neumann, K., 73
Neuschatz, J. S., 8–9, 118, 130–31, 143–44; FAE and, 110, 114–15; incentives disclosed and, 103; informant testimony and, 11–13, 60, 67–68; safeguards tested by, 147
noncohabitating heterosexual couples, 86
nonverbal cues, 96

OBSP. *See* Old Bailey Session Papers
Office of Policy and Management, 161
Ogloff, J., 146
Oklahoma, 162
Old Bailey Session Papers (OBSP), 24
open-ended questions, 72–73, 85, 114
opponent-party statements, 39
Othello error, 90

Parisi, John, 41
Parks, M. R., 86
Pawlenko, N. B., 144
Pearcy, Jack, 98–99
peer review, 167n2 (chap.6)
Peloponnesian War, 19
Pennington, April, 123
Pennington, N., 120
People v. Gray, 13
People v. Rainge, 69
People v. Restivo, 10, 37
People v. Thompson, 2, 100
People v. Wyniemko, 10
Perez, Fernando, 33
perjury, 77, 107–8
Perkins, Lloyd, 41–42
physical arousal, 88
physical evidence, 1–2
physiological cues, 88
Pica, E., 131
plea agreement, 99
police interrogations, 1, 58, 91–92
police officers: confession judgments of, 92–94; crimes accurate details by, 11; criminal posing as, 31; deception detection by, 16; informant networks of, 18; informant testimony assisted by, 32; recordings impacting, 153–54
Porter, Lynn, 156
positive constraint, 73
prejudice, 137
pre-sentencing guidelines, 51
pretrial confessions, 28

pretrial hearings, 16, 35, 156, 158–59
Preyer, Francis, 25
primary confessions, 107; false convictions from, 65; legal decision making from, 70–71; perceptions of, 70–74; police interrogation causing, 58; secondary confession compared to, 110–11; theories of, 60–61
Proclamation 547, 22
prosecution, 119, 151–55; closing statements of, 13; common informers with successful, 21; cross-examination by, 39–40; deception detection and, 87–88; exculpatory information disclosed by, 53–54; incentives disclosure by, 124–25; informant credibility checking, 32–33; informant testimony for, 2–3, 10, 12–13; witnesses, 9; witness vetting by, 12, 14, 96–97
prosecutorial bias, 12, 119
psychoanalytic explanation, 61
psychology: of confessions, 57; experts in, 126, 156–57; of jailhouse informant, 4; research in, 16
pyramid model, 157–58

Qualtrics.com, 72

Rainge, Willie, 68
Ramsey, JonBenét, 65
rape trial, 111, 125–26
Rat Manual, 160
recordings, 153–54, 163
regulation, of informant testimony, 55
rehearsed responses, 95
Reno, Janet, 155
research, 16, 71, 100–102; of expert testimony, 133–35; field-based approach used in, 88–89, 91–92; informant testimony study for, 142–46; lab-based approach used in, 89, 92–94; social-psychological, 109; survey approach used in, 89–91

Restivo, John, 37
retributive acts, 22
Robb, A., 81
Robertson, C., 107
role-playing vignettes, 64, 71
romantic partners, 86
Ross, L., 117
Rule 801, in Federal Rules of Evidence, 39
R. v. Atwood and Robbins, 27
Ryder, Dudley, 24

safeguards, 147; for informant testimony, 5–6, 16; for witnesses receiving incentives, 136
Salaam, Yusef, 66
Sanders, Scott, 33
scientific evidence, 125–26, 131
search and seizure, 40–41
secondary confessions, 107; content of, 68; DNA evidence and, 56; false, 31; false testimony from, 66–67; incentives in, 63–64; indirect participation in, 60; informant testimony as, 5; jurors influenced by, 102; Kassin and, 157–58; motivations for, 63; paths to, 58–60; primary confession compared to, 110–11; reliability of, 101; theoretical explanations for, 62; wrongful convictions from, 129–30
self-disclosure task, 85
self-incrimination, 34, 41–42
self-regulation, 61–62
self-report data, 83
Senate Bill 156, 163
sentencing guidelines, 51–52
Serota, K. B., 81–83
sexual assault, 39, 111, 133
shame, 62
Simons, M. A., 52
simulated video trial, 146, 152
Singleton, Sonya, 50
Singleton I, 50–51

Singleton II, 50–52
situational factors, 63, 114–15
Sixth Amendment, 38, 42–43, 45, 136, 163
60 Minutes, 30–31, 60
Skalnik, Paul, 98–99
Snitching (Natapoff), 15
snitch testimony, 4, 7
social interactions, 80–81
social-psychological research, 61–62, 109
social scientists, 129, 135
Spitzer, Todd, 33
standard deviations, 105–6
State of TN v. Copeland, 157
State v. Grimes, 140
State v. Hernandez, 13
State v. Leniart, 124
State v. Patterson, 140–41
Steblay, N., 145
story model, 120–21
Strömwall, L. A., 93
strong-evidence case, 145
subjective behavior cues, 90
Sudderth, Reginald Stacy, 156–57
Sukel, H., 74
Supreme Court: *Arizona v. Fulminante* from, 73; *Brady v. Maryland* from, 52–54; *Brewer v. Williams* from, 43–44; *Brown v. Mississippi* from, 58; on Confrontation Clause, 136; *Daubert v. Merrell Dow Pharmaceuticals* from, 125–30; *Frye v. US* from, 125; *Hoffa v. US* in, 41; jailhouse informant testimony protected by, 6; *Kuhlmann v. Wilson* from, 47–49; *Kyles v. Whitley* from, 54; *Maine v. Moulton* from, 45–46; *Massiah v. US* from, 43, 45; Moulton decision upheld by, 46–47; self-incrimination ruling of, 42; *US v. Henry* from, 44–45; *US v. White* from, 41
survey method, 88–91
Surveymonkey, 72

survey research, 100–102
Swanner, J. K., 63–64, 107
Swinton, Alfred, 5, 34

Taliento, Robert, 53
Tallon, J., 120
Tardy, Bertha, 76
TDT. *See* truth-default theory
testimony, 4, 7; admissibility of, 5–6, 39–40, 145; courtroom with accuracy of, 119; discrepancies in, 12; dispositional factors in, 110; expert psychological, 125–35; eyewitness's inconsistent, 139; Federal Rules of Evidence's admissibility of, 39–40; hearsay, 38–39; incentives return for, 8; pretrial hearings for credibility of, 16; risks in, 14–15; truthful, 97; unreliable witness, 27–28, 77–78; of witnesses, 117. *See also* expert testimony; false testimony; informant testimony
Texas, 162
Thompson, Thomas, 2–3, 100
Title 18, Section 201(c)(2), 50
totality of circumstances, 70
tracking system, 35
transparency, of informant testimony, 162
treason, 19
trigger event, 116
Trott, Stephen, 149
truth bias, 79, 80–82, 85, 96, 115; defining, 83; empirical confirmation of, 84; explanations for, 86–87; romantic partners and, 86
truth-default theory (TDT), 83, 86–87, 115–16, 122
truthful responses, 95–97
truth-lie judgment, 85
tunnel vision, 116–19

undisclosed information, 11–12
United States, 29–30, 58

US v. Cervantes-Pacheco, 104, 140
US v. Henry, 44–46
US v. Singleton, 50, 52
US v. White, 41

Veal, Fredrick, 76–77
Vernon, Leslie, 49
video recordings, interrogations with, 91–92, 154–55
Vidocq, Eugène-François, 18, 29
Vincent, Howard, 29
violent crimes, 9
Vrij, A., 12, 94

Wallace, D. B., 74
Wason Four Card Problem, 118
Watkins, Jerry, 56
Webb, Johnny, 54
Wetmore, S. A., 15, 134, 143–44, 147; FAE studies by, 115; secondary confessions and, 110–11
Wheatcroft, J. M., 139
White, James, 41, 60, 82
White, Leslie Vernon, 30–31
Wigmore, J. H., 28
Williams, Dennis, 68
Williams, Robert, 44
Willingham, Cameron Todd, 54
Wilson, Joseph Allan, 47
Winkelman, D. A., 107
witnesses, 9, 17; credibility of, 140; cross-examination preparation by, 139–40; Crown system of, 23–28; expert, 124–25; informant, 114; jurors believing, 116; motivations of, 137; prosecution vetting of, 12, 14, 96–97; safeguards against compensated, 136; testimony of, 117; unreliable, 27–28, 77–78
Woody, W. D., 133
Wrightsman, L. S., 73

Zimmerman, C., 20–21

ABOUT THE AUTHORS

JEFFREY S. NEUSCHATZ, PhD, is Professor of Psychology at the University of Alabama in Huntsville. His primary research interests include eyewitness memory, lineup identification, secondary confessions, and jury decision making. In terms of eyewitness identification, he has been concerned with two primary areas: show-up identification and post-identification feedback. His work on show-up identification has focused on factors that influence its reliability. He has pioneered research on jailhouse informant testimony. He has published over fifty articles and chapters. In addition, he has co-authored a book, *The Psychology of Eyewitness Identification* (2012).

JONATHAN M. GOLDING is Professor of Psychology at the University of Kentucky. His research concerns legal decision making and various aspects of memory (child and elder eyewitness memory, repressed memory, DNA evidence, hearsay testimony, demeanor of witnesses, type of crime disclosure, type of crime, and the impact of courtroom experts). His work has led to numerous publications in scientific journals and books. He has served as an expert reviewer for numerous journals, including *Law and Human Behavior, Psychology, Crime and Law, Child Abuse & Neglect, Child Maltreatment, Criminal Justice and Behavior,* and *Psychology, Public Policy & Law*.

Lightning Source UK Ltd.
Milton Keynes UK
UKHW011946030222
398167UK00002B/154